GODWIN & MARY

GODWIN

*Letters of William Godwin
and Mary Wollstonecraft*

UNIVERSITY OF NEBRASKA PRESS

& MARY

edited by RALPH M. WARDLE

LINCOLN AND LONDON

Publishers on the Plains

UNP

© Copyright 1966 by the University of Kansas Press

First Bison Book printing: 1977

Library of Congress Cataloging in Publication Data

Godwin, William, 1756–1836.
    Godwin & Mary.

    Reprint of the ed. published by University of Kansas Press,
Lawrence.
    Includes bibliographical references.
    1. Godwin, William, 1756–1836—Correspondence.
2. Wollstonecraft, Mary, 1759–1797—Correspondence.
I. Wollstonecraft, Mary, 1759–1797. II. Wardle, Ralph Martin,
1909–   ed. III. Title.
[PR4723.G6 1976]   828'.6'09 [B]   76–13032
ISBN 0–8032–0901–0
ISBN 0–8032–5852–6 pbk.

Bison Book edition reprinted by arrangement with the University
of Kansas Press

Manufactured in the United States of America

PREFACE

After the death of Mary Wollstonecraft in 1797 her husband, William Godwin, sought distraction from his bereavement by preparing her surviving papers for publication. The *Posthumous Works of the Author of "A Vindication of the Rights of Woman,"* which was published by Joseph Johnson in 1798, contained, in addition to several works that she had left unfinished, a series of sixteen letters written to Johnson and another of seventy-seven addressed to the American Gilbert Imlay, who had been Mary's lover before her marriage to Godwin.[1] The 162 known letters which had passed between Mary and himself before and after their marriage in March, 1797, Godwin understandably withheld from publication. Instead he arranged them in chronological order, supplied dates for most of them, and stored them among his private papers.

At his death his papers passed to his daughter, Mary Shelley, who in turn left them to her son, Sir Percy Shelley. After the death of Sir Percy and his wife the manuscript materials in their possession were divided into three lots: one went to the Bodleian Library, a second to Sir Percy's heir (and eventually bequeathed to the Bodleian), and the third to Lady Shelley's niece, Bessie Florence (Gibson) Scarlett, mother of the fifth Lord Abinger. At the present time this third lot, composed in part of Godwin's Journal and his and his wife's letters, is housed at Clees Hall, Bures, Suffolk, the residence of the eighth Lord Abinger.

Of the original 160 letters which Godwin preserved, nine (1, 16, 43, 62, 100, 122, 124, 155, 156) are missing from

---

[1] Later editions of the Letters to Imlay were issued by Kegan Paul in 1879 and by Roger Ingpen in 1908.

Lord Abinger's collection, and a careful search of other libraries and collections has failed to reveal them. There are, however, two others in the Abinger Collection which are not numbered or dated: one a seventeen-word note from Godwin, the other a longer note from Mary which Godwin seems to have regarded as a continuation of Letter 106. I have included and discussed both in the Appendix.

Of the 151 letters printed in the body of the text, twenty-seven (90-92, 96, 98, 104, 106, 108-109, 111-112, 116, 118-121, 127, 131-136, 138, 158-160) and parts of five others (113, 123, 128-130) were printed, often inaccurately, in Kegan Paul's *William Godwin: His Friends and Contemporaries* (2 vols., London, 1876); seventeen others (2, 4, 6-7, 12-13, 19-20, 31, 45-46, 51, 59, 66-67, 87-88) and parts of twenty-four more (3, 5, 14, 18, 23-24, 32, 35, 40, 52-53, 63-64, 68-69, 71, 75-77, 80, 82-83, 140, 153) were included in my *Mary Wollstonecraft: A Critical Biography* (Lawrence, Kansas, and London, 1951); and one note (154) and part of another (39) are quoted in *Shelley and His Circle* (ed. Kenneth Neill Cameron, 2 vols., Cambridge, Massachusetts, and London, 1961). The present collection, therefore, contains seventy-six pieces published for the first time and, in addition, thirty never before completely printed.

It is a remarkably complete correspondence. Even after they were married Godwin and Mary made a point of living separate lives: he went every day to nearby rooms to write, and they often spent their evenings each with his own circle of friends. Yet they were unusually articulate people, they kept in close touch with each other, and they seem to have preserved all the communications that passed between them from the beginning of their courtship in July, 1796, until the very day of Mary's fatal confinement in August, 1797. Her notes outnumber Godwin's—perhaps because he was the more systematic about preserving correspondence, perhaps because her more volatile nature was quicker to overflow in writing.

The letters are transcribed here substantially as they were written—with only the most obvious slips of the pen corrected. Godwin's letters would demand little alteration from the most puristic of editors, but Mary's could profit—in clarity at least—from frequent emendations. Yet it has seemed best to transcribe them as she wrote them, since her haphazard punctuation and sentence structure and her reckless use of the dash, though sometimes confusing, are often an index to the state of her mind. And they suggest a good deal about her impetuous nature, so different from, yet so complementary to, her impassive husband's.

The dates given in brackets at the head of most of the letters are those added to the manuscripts by Godwin. Undoubtedly they can be accepted as reliable, since he supplied them only a few months after the composition of the letters and since he had his Journal to remind him of related events. Some of the letters left undated were obviously written within hours of those which immediately precede them. In such cases I have supplied no date; in fact, throughout both text and notes I have sought to interfere as little as possible. Godwin and Mary can best tell their own story.

I am again deeply indebted to Lord Abinger for his kindness in permitting me to transcribe and publish the letters. I wish also to acknowledge the aid given me by Mr. William R. Maidment, Librarian of the London Borough of Camden, Professor Jack W. Marken of Pennsylvania State College at Slippery Rock, Professor Burton R. Pollin of Bronx Community College, and the officers and staffs of the Ashmolean Museum, the Birmingham (England) Public Libraries, the British Museum, the Library of Harvard University, the National Portrait Gallery, and the University of Omaha Library. Thanks also are due to Professor Carl R. Woodring of Columbia University and Professor Clyde K. Hyder and Dean William P. Albrecht of the University of Kansas, who read the manuscript and offered many helpful suggestions. But as always, my greatest debt and gratitude are to Mary E. Wardle, who has cheerfully shared the rewarding labor of preparing these letters for the press.

R. M. W.

University of Omaha
February, 1966

Contents

Illustrations

INTRODUCTION

One Friday evening in January, 1796, Miss Mary Hays, an eager little woman who clung to the fringes of London radical society, entertained a group of serious thinkers at her rooms in Hatton Gardens. Among her guests were two—William Godwin and Mary Wollstonecraft—who were rightly considered among the brightest luminaries of the circle which Miss Hays cultivated. They had met before—back in November, 1791, when both were little better than literary hacks. Godwin, by that time, had renounced the Unitarian ministry and was writing regularly for the *Annual Register;* but he had not yet published his *Enquiry Concerning Political Justice,* the book which shocked England with its theory of philosophical anarchism. As for Mary, she had written one book which had attracted notice: *A Vindication of the Rights of Men,* a reply to Edmund Burke's *Reflections on the Revolution in France.* But most of her literary efforts had been confined to translating, compiling children's books, or writing articles for the monthly *Analytical Review.*

That first meeting had hardly been auspicious. Tom Paine had been present, and Godwin had looked forward to hearing his opinions on several topics of mutual interest. But poor Paine had scarcely had a chance to open his mouth. Whatever subject was broached, Miss Wollstonecraft, with all the self-assurance of one who has had her first taste of success, spoke up at once, and declared her opinions so copiously—and often so acrimoniously—that Godwin had left the party with little desire to know her better. They had met occasionally in the year that intervened before Mary left for Paris to witness the French

1

Revolution at first hand; but they had made, as he later reported, "a very small degree of progress towards a cordial acquaintance."

Miss Hays seems to have known that the two were far from congenial, and she evidently considered it only fair, when she invited Godwin, to warn him that Mrs. Wollstonecraft (as she had been called since the publication of her famous *Vindication of the Rights of Woman* in 1792) would be present. But Godwin, secure in his position as author of the impressive *Political Justice* and the popular novel *Caleb Williams,* refused to be intimidated. "I will do myself the pleasure of waiting on you on Friday," he wrote in reply to the invitation, "& shall be happy to meet Mrs. Wolstencraft, of whom I know not that I ever said a word of harm, & who has frequently amused herself with depreciating me. But I trust you acknowledge in me the reality of a habit upon which I pique myself, that I speak of the qualities of others uninfluenced by personal considerations, & am as prompt to do justice to an enemy as to a friend." When Friday evening came around and he met Mary again, he found to his surprise that she no longer seemed so offensive. "Sympathy in her anguish," he wrote later, "added in my mind to the respect I had always entertained for her talents."

Mary had certainly changed since 1791—and not without reason. She had suffered disappointment after disappointment, and they had given depth to her character and softness to her manners. Her first shock had come soon after the publication of her *Rights of Woman,* when she fell in love with the artist Henry Fuseli and begged his wife to allow her to live as a member of their family—only to be forbidden ever to enter their house again. In despair

2

she had gone off to France, hoping "to lose in public happiness the sense of private sorrow." But before her visit ended, England declared war on France, and she found herself suddenly stranded, an enemy alien, in a bloodthirsty city. Then one day she met a dashing American named Gilbert Imlay, with whom she fell violently in love. She became his mistress, bore him a daughter, and dreamed of settling with him on a farm in the New World, where they would live happily forever. But gradually she perceived that Imlay's love was cooling. Business called him away from home for weeks at a time. She followed him first to Le Havre, then back to London. And there, in despair, she attempted suicide. She was discovered and prevented, and Imlay dispatched her to Scandinavia to attend to his business affairs. Off she went, driven by the hope that she might regain his affection by serving him. But his letters to her were few and cold; and, on her return to London, she discovered that he was living with another woman. Then once again she attempted suicide, and once again she was rescued. And when Godwin met her at Miss Hays's party she was striving to reconcile herself to her fate.

She was certainly not looking for a husband; in fact, she was presently to make a final effort to win Imlay back. But though he seemed at times to have decided not to break with her altogether, she realized at last that no appeal from her could reach his heart. And two months after her meeting with Godwin she wrote Imlay her last letter. "I part with you in peace," she concluded; and from that time onward she armed herself to stifle every trace of the old love.

3

By the beginning of April she had taken lodgings on Cumming Street, in Pentonville, not far from Godwin's house on Chalton Street in Somers Town. She intended to stay there only temporarily—long enough to earn the money needed to transport herself and her little daughter to Italy or Switzerland. But on April 14, apparently without invitation, she called on Godwin at his house. He must have been startled at her audacity, but he was certainly not displeased. Since their last meeting he had taken time to read her *Letters Written during a Short Residence in Sweden, Norway, and Denmark,* and it had confirmed the favorable impression which he had received at Miss Hays's party. A week later, on April 22, he entertained her at a gala dinner at his house, along with several of his most distinguished friends: Dr. Samuel Parr, Mrs. Eliza-beth Inchbald, Thomas Holcroft, and James Mackintosh.

Soon Godwin was courting with zest. This was not his first experience of the sort: he had, in recent months, been making advances to two literary ladies, Mrs. Inchbald and Amelia Alderson. The role of suitor did not come easily to him, but he persevered. He even composed a poetical tribute to Mary, and her acknowledgment of it showed that she was a bit amused at his gallantry—and, evidently, determined not to repay his flattery in kind:

I send you the last volume of 'Héloïse', because, if you have it not, you may chance to wish for it. You may perceive by this remark that I do not give you credit for as much philosophy as our friend [Rousseau], and I want besides to remind you, when you write to me in *verse,* not to choose the easiest task, my perfections, but to dwell on your own feelings—that is to say, give me a bird's-eye view of your heart. Do not make me a desk 'to write upon,' I humbly pray—unless you honestly acknowledge yourself *bewitched.*

4

Of that I shall judge by the style in which the eulogiums flow, for I think I have observed that you compliment without rhyme or reason, when you are almost at a loss what to say.[1]

During the month of July Godwin made a trip down to his native county of Norfolk. While he was gone Mary gave up her rooms on Cumming Street and moved to a house at No. 16 Judd Place West, on the outskirts of Somers Town. "Probably without knowing exactly why," Godwin wrote in his *Memoirs* of Mary, she had abandoned her plan to settle on the Continent; in fact she had taken out of storage the furniture which had been in a London warehouse ever since her departure for France in 1792.

On July 10 Godwin called at Dr. Alderson's house in Norwich and, as his Journal records, proposed to the Doctor's daughter Amelia. Evidently he was given no encouragement, for three days later, still in Norwich, he wrote the letter which begins this collection.

This time his advances were more warmly received. Mary may have been amused at her suitor's clumsy efforts to be courtly, but she was clearly touched by his open declaration—and his wry manner of making it. She was already half-won, and by mid-August, three weeks after Godwin's return to London, they were lovers.

From that time onward the letters can tell, almost unaided, the story of how their affair developed into an enduring love. Its course did not always run smooth. Mary was apprehensive: Had she yielded too easily to her lover? Would he tire of her as Imlay had done? Pregnancy sharpened her fears and her irritability. Yet Godwin did

---

[1] Ford K. Brown, *Life of William Godwin,* London and Toronto, 1926, p. 116. I have been unable to locate the original of this letter, which Brown dates July 1, 1796, without giving its source. It is probably the Letter 1 missing from the Abinger Collection. (See discussion above, pp. v-vi.)

not fail her, and gradually her impetuous nature grew calmer, her shattered nerves were soothed. She in turn sparked the warmth that lay hidden beneath the frosty surface of her philosopher-lover. Eventually they decided that wedlock would not be so confining as they had supposed; and on March 29, 1797, the man who had pronounced marriage "an affair of property—and the worst of properties" was duly wedded at St. Pancras Church to the woman who had once exulted when she gave herself to another lover "without having clogged my soul by promising obedience &c &c."

Of course their troubles did not end at the altar: Mary was now annoyed that her husband failed to assume the proper responsibilities of the head of a household, now alarmed when a Miss Pinkerton seemed to be demanding too much of Godwin's attention. But she had no reason to question his loyalty. He catered to her whims, he did his best to talk her language, and, most important, he stood ever firm and constant in his love. Marriage was not a perfect state, perhaps, but it was a blessed one. And when they were temporarily separated by a visit which Godwin paid to his friends the Wedgwoods in Etruria, Mary acknowledged that "a husband is a convenient part of the furniture of a house," and Godwin replied that "after all one's philosophy, it must be confessed that the knowledge, that there is someone that takes an interest in our happiness . . . is extremely gratifying."

The letters reach a poignant climax in the three brave notes which Mary wrote while she cheerfully awaited the momentary arrival of "little William"—who proved to be a little Mary. The tragic sequel—Mary's last illness and

6

death—is stoically recorded in the final chapter of Godwin's *Memoirs* of Mary.

When he published the agonized series of letters which Mary had written to Gilbert Imlay, Godwin observed in his preface that the collection "may possibly be found to contain the finest examples of the language of sentiment and passion ever presented to the world." His own letters to Mary, and hers to him, he withheld from the public. But surely they have more appeal for most readers; for in them we hear not one voice crying in a void, but two people conversing intimately—two quite different people, a man and a woman, both by nature independent, both individualists, but gradually developing a love that was all that love between man and woman should be: a combination of tender consideration and mutual respect, heightened by moments of fiery passion—a love that fused two human beings into one couple.

Each was a stronger and better person for the fusion; each found through it fulfillment—a fulfillment which Mary had long sought in vain and which Godwin had never before known to exist.

2. GODWIN TO MARY
July 13, 1796[1]

By way of discharging a debt, an obligation, what shall I say, I take up the pen.

Oh No! exclaimeth Mary, tant soit peu piqué, it is a mere task then, is it?

Now, I take all my Gods to witness—do you know how many they are?—but I obtest & obsecrate them all—that your company infinitely delights me, that I love your imagination, your delicate epicurism, the malicious leer of your eye,[2] in short every thing that constitutes the bewitching tout ensemble of the celebrated Mary. But to write!

Alas, I have no talent, for I have no subject. Shall I write a love letter? May Lucifer fly away with me, if I do! No, when I make love, it shall be with the eloquent tones of my voice, with dying accents, with speaking glances (through the glass of my spectacles), with all the witching of that irresistible, universal passion. Curse on the mechanical, icy medium of pen & paper. When I make love, it shall be in a storm, as Jupiter made love to Semele, & turned her at once to a cinder. Do not these menaces terrify you?

Well then, what shall be my subject. Shall I send you an eulogium of your beauty, your talents & your virtues? Ah! that is an old subject: beside, if I were to begin, instead of a sheet of paper, I should want a ream.

Shall I write to citizenness Wolstencraft a congratulatory epistle upon the victories of Buonaparti?[3] That I may rejoice the cockles of her heart, shall I cause once more to pass in review before her the Saint Jerome, the Santa Cecilia,[4] & the other inestimable treasures, of which that

8

ferocious freebooter has robbed the classical & delicious cities of Italy?

Invent me a subject against my return, &, the next time I go into the country, I will write you such a letter!

Cause Margaret[5] to drop a line into my letter box, signifying to the janitor, or jailor, Mr. Marshal,[6] that I expect to arrive on this day sevennight at seven o'clock in the morning, to depart no more.

Thus much by these presents from,

Your admirer,
W Godwin

Norwich
July 13. 1796.

1. This letter is the earliest of those now preserved in the Abinger Collection. The letter Godwin numbered 1 may be Mary's letter to him dated July 1, 1796, quoted in the Introduction, pp. 4-5.

2. Cf. Robert Southey's letter to Joseph Cottle dated March 13, 1797: "Perhaps you will be surprised to hear that, of all the lions or *literati* that I have seen here, there is not one whose countenance has not some unpleasant trait. Mary Imlay's is the best, infinitely the best; the only fault in it is an expression . . . indicating superiority; not haughtiness, not sarcasm in Mary Imlay, but still it is unpleasant. Her eyes are light brown, and, though the lid of one of them is affected by a little paralysis, they are the most meaning I ever saw."—Quoted in F. K. Brown, *Life of William Godwin,* London and Toronto, 1926, pp. 117-118.

3. In April and May of 1796 Napoleon had enjoyed a series of military victories over the Austrians and Piedmontese, followed by a series of "truces" with Italian duchies and (in June) with the Pope.

4. Raphael's *St. Cecilia* and Agustino Carracci's *Communion of St. Jerome* were among the art treasures carried by Napoleon from Bologna to Paris. They were returned to Bologna in 1815.

5. Godwin doubtless refers to the nurse Marguerite whom Mary had brought from France in 1795.

6. James Marshal, the literary hack who shared Godwin's house on Chalton Street, Somers Town.

3. MARY TO GODWIN
[July 21, 1796]

I send you, as requested, the altered M.S.[1] Had you called upon me yesterday I should have thanked you for your letter—and—perhaps, have told you that the sentence I *liked* best was the concluding one, where you tell me, that you were coming home, to depart *no more*—But now I am out of humour I mean to bottle up my kindness, unless something in your countenance, when I do see you, should make the cork fly out—whether I will or not.—

Mary—

Thursday
Judd Place West

1. Apparently the manuscript of one of Mary's works in progress; perhaps *The Wrongs of Woman; or, Maria,* which she left unfinished at her death. Godwin published the extant fragments in Volumes I and II of *Posthumous Works of the Author of "A Vindication of the Rights of Woman"* (4 vols., London, 1798).

4. MARY TO GODWIN
[July 26, 1796]

The weather not allowing me to go out about business to day, as I intended, if you are disengaged, I and my *habit* are at your service, in spite of wind or weather—

Mary—

Tuesday—

5. MARY TO GODWIN
[August 2, 1796]

From the style of the note, in which your epistle was enveloped, Miss Hays[1] seems *plus triste que ordinaire*. Have you seen her?

I suppose you mean to drink tea with me, *one* of these day[s]—How can you find in your heart to let me pass so many evenings alone—you may saucily ask, why I do not send for Mr. Twiss[2]—but I shall reply with dignity—No; there will be more dignity in silence—so mum.

I did not wish to see you this evening, because you have been dining, I suppose, with Mrs. Perfection,[3] and comparison[s] are odious

1. Mary Hays, the woman who had brought Godwin and Mary together in January, 1796. She seems to have cultivated an interesting sadness because of a disappointment in love which she was presently to record for posterity in her novel *Emma Courtney* (London, 1796). Cf. *The Love-Letters of Mary Hays (1779-1780)*, ed. A. F. Wedd, London, 1925.

2. Francis Twiss, author of a concordance to Shakespeare's

plays, who married Frances (Fanny) Kemble, sister of Mrs. Siddons.

3. Mary probably refers to the novelist Elizabeth Inchbald, whom Godwin had been courting. As Mary reveals in Letter 32, below, she was not at first attracted to the lady.

6. MARY TO GODWIN
[August 4, 1796]

I spent the evening with Mademoiselle Alderson[1]—you, I'm told, were ready to devour her—in your little parlour. Elle est tres jolie—n'est pas? I was making a question yesterday, as I talked to myself, whether Cymons of forty[2] could be *informed*—Perhaps, after last nights electrical shock, you can resolve me—

1. Amelia Alderson, the youthful novelist from Norwich who later married the painter John Opie. Mary clearly regarded her, like Mrs. Inchbald, as a potential rival for Godwin's attentions.
2. In Boccaccio's *Decameron* (Fifth Day, First Novel) the brutish Cymon is transformed into a polished gentleman by his love for the beautiful Iphigenia.

7. MARY TO GODWIN
[August 6, 1796]

Miss Alderson was wondering, this morning whether you *ever* kissed a maiden fair—As you do not like to solve problems, *on paper*, TELL her *before* you part—She will tell *me* next—year—[1]

1. This letter was addressed in Mary's hand "To Willm. Godwin Philosopher" with the direction: "Not to be opened 'till the

12

Philosopher has been an hour at least, in Miss Alderson's company, cheek by jowl."

8. MARY TO GODWIN
[August 7, 1796]

I supped in company with Mrs Siddons,[1] last night. When shall I tell you what I think of her?—

1. Sarah Siddons, the celebrated "Tragic Muse," was a close friend of Mary's at this time.

9. MARY TO GODWIN
[August 11, 1796]

Won'tee, as Fannikin[1] would say, come and see me to day? and I will go home with you to hear your essays,[2] should you chance to be awake. I called on you yesterday, in my way to dinner, not for Mary—but *to bring* Mary[3]—Is it necessary to tell your sapient Philosophership that I mean MYSELF—

1. Mary's pet name for Fanny, her two-year-old daughter by the American Gilbert Imlay.
2. Godwin and Mary were reading the manuscript of Godwin's *The Enquirer,* which was published early in 1797.
3. The first *Mary* may refer either to Mary's servant of that name or to the semiautobiographical novel which Mary had written in 1787 and which Joseph Johnson published in 1788.

10. GODWIN TO MARY
August 16, 1796

I have been very unwell all night. You did not consider me enough in that way yesterday, & therefore unintentionally impressed upon me a mortifying sensation. When you see me next; will you condescend to take me for better for worse, that is, be prepared to find me, as it shall happen, full of gaiety & life, or a puny valetudinarian? Farewel, remember our agreement!

Tuesday / Augst. 16th

11. MARY TO GODWIN
[August 16, 1796]

I send you the new[sp]aper before the hour, because I suppose you will go out earlier than usual today.

Give Churchhill[1] to Fanny if you can spare him, and, you may kiss her, if you please.

Entre nous—did you feel very lonely last night?

1. Mary probably refers to one of the works of the satirist Charles Churchill, author of *The Rosciad* (1761), *The Prophecy of Famine* (1763), etc.

12. MARY TO GODWIN
[August 17, 1796]

I have not lately passed so painful a night as the last. I feel that I cannot speak clearly on the subject to you, let me then briefly explain myself now I am alone.

14

Yet, struggling as I have been a long time to attain peace of mind (or apathy) I am afraid to trace emotions to their source, which border on agony.

Is it not sufficient to tell you that I am thoroughly out of humour with myself? Mortified and humbled, I scarcely know why—still, despising false delicacy I almost fear that I have lost sight of the true. Could a wish have transported me to France or Italy, last night, I should have caught up my Fanny and been off in a twinkle, though convinced that it is my mind, not the place, which requires changing. My imagination is for ever betraying me into fresh misery, and I perceive that I shall be a child to the end of the chapter. You talk of the roses which grow profusely in every path of life—I catch at them; but only encounter the thorns.—

I would not be unjust for the world—I can only say that you appear to me to have acted injudiciously; and that full of your own feelings, little as I comprehend them, you forgot mine—or do not understand my character. It is my turn to have a fever to day—I am not well—I am hurt—But I mean not to hurt you. Consider what has passed as a fever of your imagination; one of the slight mortal shakes to which you are liable—and I—will become again a *Solitary Walker*. Adieu! I was going to add God bless you!—[1]

Wednesday Morning

1. This and the three following letters seem to have been occasioned by Mary's qualms after she and Godwin became lovers. In his *Memoirs of the Author of "A Vindication of the Rights of Woman"* (ed. W. Clark Durant, London and New York, 1927, p.

100) Godwin states that their love was first acknowledged three weeks after his return from Norwich. The cryptic entries "chez moi" and "chez elle" in Godwin's Journal begin on August 15 and 18 respectively.

13. GODWIN TO MARY
[August 17, 1796]

How shall I answer you? In one point we sympathize; I had rather at this moment talk to you on paper than in any other mode. I should feel ashamed in seeing you.

You do not know how honest I am. I swear to you that I told you nothing but the strict & literal truth, when I described to you the manner in which you set my imagination on fire on Saturday. For six & thirty hours I could think of nothing else. I longed inexpressibly to have you in my arms. Why did not I come to you? I am a fool. I feared still that I might be deceiving myself as to your feelings, & that I was feeding my mind with groundless presumptions. I determined to suffer the point to arrive at its own denouement. I was not aware that the fervour of my imagination was exhausting itself. Yet this, I believe, is no uncommon case.

Like any other man, I can speak only of what I know. But this I can boldly affirm, that nothing that I have seen in you would in the slightest degree authorise the opinion, that, *in despising the false delicacy, you have lost sight of the true*. I see nothing in you but what I respect & adore.

I know the acuteness of your feelings, & there is perhaps nothing upon earth that would give me so pungent a remorse, as to add to your unhappiness.

16

Do not hate me. Indeed I do not deserve it. Do not cast me off. Do not become again a *solitary walker*. Be just to me, & then, though you will discover in me much that is foolish and censurable, yet a woman of your understanding will still regard me with some partiality.

Upon consideration I find in you one fault, & but one. You have the feelings of nature, & you have the honesty to avow them. In all this you do well. I am sure you do. But do not let them tyrannise over you. Estimate every thing at its just value. It is best that we should be friends in every sense of the word; but in the mean time let us be friends.

Suffer me to see you. Let us leave every thing else to its own course. My imagination is not dead, I suppose, though it sleeps. But, be it as it will, I will torment you no more. I will be your friend, the friend of your mind, the admirer of your excellencies. All else I commit to the disposition of futurity, glad, if completely happy; passive & silent in this respect, while I am not so.

Be happy. Resolve to be happy. You deserve to be so. Every thing that interferes with it, is weakness & wandering; & a woman, like you, can, must, shall, shake it off. Afford, for instance, no food for the morbid madness, & no triumph to the misanthropical gloom, of your afternoon visitor.[1] Call up, with firmness, the energies, which, I am sure, you so eminently possess.

Send me word that I may call on you in a day or two. Do you not see, while I exhort you to be a philosopher, how painfully acute are my own feelings? I need some soothing, though I cannot ask it from you.

Wednesday

1. Mary Hays. (See below, Letter 14: "Miss H— seldom stays late, never to supper. . . .")

14. MARY TO GODWIN
[August 17, 1796]

I like your last—may I call it *love* letter? better than the first—and can I give you a higher proof of my esteem than to tell you, the style of my letter will whether I will or no, that it has calmed my mind—a mind that had been painfully active all the morning, haunted by old sorrows that seemed to come forward with new force to sharpen the present anguish—Well! well—it is almost gone—I mean all my unreasonable fears—and a whole train of tormentors, which you have routed—I can scarcely describe to you their ugly shapes so quickly do they vanish —and let them go, we will not bring them back by talking of them. You may see me when you please. I shall take this letter, just before dinner time, to ask you to come and dine with me, and Fanny, whom I have shut out to day. Should you be engaged come in the evening. Miss H— seldom stays late, never to supper—or to morrow—as you wish—I shall be content—You say you want soothing— will it sooth you to tell you the truth? I cannot hate you— I do not think you deserve it. Nay, more I cannot withhold my friendship from you, and will try to merit yours, that *necessity* may bind you to me.

One word of my ONLY fault—our imaginations have been rather differently employed—I am more of a painter than you—I like to tell the truth, my taste for the picturesque has been more cultivated—I delight to view the

18

grand scenes of nature and the various changes of the human countenance—Beautiful as they are animated by intelligence or sympathy—My affections have been more exercised than yours, I believe, and my senses are quick, without the aid of fancy—yet tenderness always prevails, which inclines me to be angry with myself, when I do not animate and please those I [love?].

Now will you not be a good boy, and smile upon me, I dine at half past four—you ought to come and give me an appetite for my dinner, as you deprived me of one for my breakfast.

Mary

Two O'Clock

15. GODWIN TO MARY
[August 17, 1796]

I left a letter for you at one o'clock. It was not till two hours later, that I suddenly became awake, & perceived the mistake I had made. Intent upon an idea I had formed in my own mind of furtive pleasure, I was altogether stupid & without intelligence as to your plan of staying, which it was morally impossible should not have given life to the dead.

Perhaps you will not believe that I could have been so destitute of understanding. It seems indeed incredible. I think however you will admit, that it is no proof of indifference to a subject, when a man's thoughts are so obstinately occupied by one view of it, that, though you were to blow a trumpet in his ear, you would not succeed in giving him an apprehension of any other.

I have now only left to apologise for my absurdity, which I do even with self-abhorrence. The mistake being detected, it is for you to decide whether it is too late to repair it. For my own part, I have not the presumption to offer even a word to implore your forgiveness.

Wednesday

I had written the above before you called. I hesitate now whether to deliver it. You say you are calmed, & I would not for the world change that state of mind for a state of anguish. My disposition however to utter all I think decides me. Take no notice of it for the present.

17. MARY TO GODWIN
[August 19, 1796]

As I was walking with Fanny this morning, before breakfast, I found a pretty little fable,[1] directly in my path; and, now I have finished my review,[2] I will transcribe it for thee.

A poor Sycamore growing up amidst a cluster of Evergreens, every time the wind beat through her slender branches, envied her neighbours the foliage which sheltered them from each cutting blast. And the only comfort this poor trembling shrub could find in her mind (as mind is *proved* to be only thought,[3] let it be taken for granted that she had a mind, if not a soul) was to say, Well; spring will come soon, and I too shall have leaves. But so impatient was this silly plant that the sun could not glisten on the snow, without her asking, of her more experienced neighbours, if this was not spring? At length the snow began to melt away, the snow-drops appeared, and the crocus did not lag long behind, the hepaticas next ventured forth, and the mezereon began to bloom.

The sun was warm—balsamic as May's own beams. Now said the sycamore, her sap mounting, as she spoke, I am sure this is spring.

Wait only for such another day, said a fading Laurel; and a weather-beaten Pine nodded, to enforce the remonstrance.

The Sycamore was not headstrong, and promised, at least, to wait for the morrow, before she burst her rind.

What a to morrow came! The sun darted forth with redoubled ardour; the winds were hushed. A gentle breeze fluttered the trees; it was the sweet southern gale, which Willy Shakespear[4] felt, and came to rouse the violets; whilst every genial zephyr gave birth to a primrose.

The Sycamore no longer regarded admonition. She felt that it was spring; and her buds, fostered by the kindest beams immediately came forth to revel in existence.

Alas! Poor Sycamore! The morrow a hoar frost covered the trees, and shrivelled up thy unfolding leaves, changing, in a moment the colour of the living green—a brown, melancholy hue succeeded—and the Sycamore drooped, abashed; whilst a taunting neighbour whispered to her, bidding her, in future, learn to distinguish february from April.—

Whether the buds recovered, and expanded, when the spring actually arrived—The Fable sayeth not—

1. Mary probably meant her fable to tell allegorically the story of her recent recovery from grief at Imlay's abandonment—and her fear that Godwin might treat her in similar fashion.

2. Mary was reviewing books for the monthly *Analytical Review*. Her only contribution to the issue for August, 1796, was a review of Fanny Burney's *Camilla*.

3. Mary added in a footnote to the letter: "See Godwin's Political Justice." She doubtless meant to refer to Book II, Chapter VII, of the book: "Of the Mechanism of the Human Mind."

4. Mary's words echo no specific passage in Shakespeare. She might have had either *Cymbeline,* IV. ii. 172, or *Twelfth Night,* I. i. 5-7, in mind.

18. GODWIN TO MARY
[August 19, 1796]

I have no answer to make to your fable, which I acknowledge to be uncommonly ingenious & well composed. I see not however its application, either to Wednesday when Miss Hayes came, & when, as you confess, my visit gave you spirits, or to yesterday, when the presence of Margaret in the next room tortured me. I had no reason to regard her as your confident, & was at a loss how to judge. Your fable of to day puts an end to all my hopes. I needed soothing, & you threaten me. Oppressed with a diffidence & uncertainty which I hate, you join the oppressors, & annihilate me. Use your pleasure. For every pain I have undesignedly given you, I am most sincerely grieved; for the good qualities I discern in you, you shall live for ever embalmed in my memory.

Friday

19. MARY TO GODWIN
[August 22, 1796]

I am sometimes painfully humble—Write me, but a line, just to assure me, that you have been thinking of me with affection, now and then—Since we parted—

20. GODWIN TO MARY
[August 22, 1796]

Humble! for heaven's sake, be proud, be arrogant! You are—but I cannot tell what you are. I cannot yet find the circumstance about you that allies you to the frailty of our nature. I will hunt it out.

21. MARY TO GODWIN
[August 24, 1796]

As you are to dine with Mrs. Perfection[1] to day, it would be dangerous, not to remind you of my existence—perhaps—a word then in your ear—should you forget, for a moment, a possible *accident* with the most delightful woman in the world, your fealty, take care not to look over your left shoulder—I shall be there—Wednesday

1. See note 3, Letter 5, above.

22. GODWIN TO MARY
[undated]

I will report my fealty this evening. Till then farewell.

23. MARY TO GODWIN
[August 26, 1796]

I seem to want encouragement—I therefore send you my M.S.[1] though not all I have written. Say when—or where, I am to see you Godwin.

Friday

1. See note 1, Letter 3, above.

24. MARY TO GODWIN
[August 27, 1796]

The wind whistles through my trees.

What do you say to our walk?

Should the weather continue uncertain *suppose* you were to bring your tragedy[1] here—and we shall be so snug —yet, you are such a kind creature, that I am afraid to express a preference, lest you should think of pleasing me rather than yourself— and is it not the same thing?—for I am never so well pleased with myself, as when I please you —I am not sure that please is the exact word to explain my sentiments—May I trust you to search in your own heart for the proper one?

Mary

Saturday Morning

1. Mary might have been referring to Godwin's *Antonio*, first produced on December 13, 1799, but begun "at least three years" earlier (Brown, *William Godwin*, p. 183). More likely, however, she had in mind *The Iron Chest*, the dramatization of Godwin's *Caleb Williams* by George Colman the Younger, which was first played in 1796. (Note the later reference to *The Iron Chest* in Letter 29, below.)

25. MARY TO GODWIN
[August 29, 1796]

I will come and dine with you to day, at half past four or five. You shall read your tragedy to me, & drive clear out of my mind all the sensations of *disgust,* which I brought home with me last night.

Twiss put you out of conceit with women, and he led my imagination to trace the fables of the Satyrs[1] to their source.

Mary

Monday

1. There seem to be no specific fables concerning the satyrs. Mary perhaps means that Twiss reminds her of the existence of creatures which are half human and half goat.

26. GODWIN TO MARY
[undated]

Your proposal meets with the wish of my heart: I called at half after two yesterday to obtain this point from you.

27. MARY TO GODWIN
[August 30, 1796]

I send no Amulet to day: but beware of enchantments—

Give Fanny a biscuit—I want you to love each other—

28. MARY TO GODWIN
[August 30, 1796]

The weather, I believe, from the present appearance will not permit me to go out to dinner—If so you will call on me in your way home—will you not? You need not write—I shall take it for granted—

29. MARY TO GODWIN
[August 31, 1796]

Since you think that I mean to cheat you I send you a family present, given me, when I was let loose in the world—Look at the first page and return it—I do not intend to let you extend your skepticism to me—or you will fright away a poor weary bird who, taking refuge in your bosom, hoped to nestle there—to the end of the chapter.

The day is dreary. The Iron Chest must wait—Will you read your piece at your fire side or mine? And I will tell you in what aspect I think you a *little* unjust.

On second thoughts, I believe, I had better drink tea with you; but then I shall not stay late.

Yours,

Mary

Wednesday—

30. MARY TO GODWIN
[undated]

This evening, dear Godwin, we must alter our plan—I am not actuated by any thing like caprice—I mean to see you, and tell you why[1]

1. This letter is a fragment; the bottom portion of the sheet has been torn away.

31. MARY TO GODWIN
[September 4, 1796]

Labouring all the morning, in vain, to overcome an oppression of spirits, which some things you uttered yesterday,[1] produced; I will try if I can shake it off by describing to you the nature of the feelings you excited.

I allude to what you remarked, relative to my manner of writing—that there was a radical defect in it—a worm in the bud—&c[2] What is to be done, I must either disregard your opinion, think it unjust, or throw down my pen in despair; and that would be tantamount to resigning existence; for at fifteen I resolved never to marry for interested motives, or to endure a life of dependence. You know not how painfully my sensibility, call it false if you will, has been wounded by some of the steps I have been obliged to take for others. I have even now plans at heart, which depend on my exertions; and my entire confidence in Mr. Imlay[3] plunged me into some difficulties, since we parted, that I could scarcely away with. I know that many of my cares have been the natural consequence of what, nine out of ten would [have] termed folly—yet I cannot coincide in the opinion, without feeling a contempt for mankind. In short, I must reckon on doing some good, and getting the money I want, by my writings, or go to sleep for ever. I shall not be content merely to keep body and soul together —By what I have already written Johnson,[4] I am sure, has been a gainer. And, for I would wish you to see my heart and mind just as it appears to myself, without drawing any veil of affected humility over it, though this whole letter is a proof of painful diffidence, I am compelled to think that there is some thing in my writings more valuable, than in the productions of some people on whom you bestow warm elogiums—I mean more mind—denominate it as you will—more of the observations of my own senses, more of the combining of my own imagination—the effusions of my own feelings and passions than the cold workings of the brain on the materials procured by the senses and imagination of other writers—

I am more out of patience with myself than you can form any idea of, when I tell you that I have scarcely written a line to please myself (and very little with respect to quantity) since you saw my M.S. I have been endeavouring all this morning; and with such dissatisfied sensations I am almost afraid to go into company—But these are idle complaints to which I ought not to give utterance, even to you—I must then have done—

Mary

Sunday Morning

1. Godwin had offended Mary by his criticism of the manuscript which he had been reading. As she reveals in Letter 40, below, Mary soon recovered from her pique and cheerfully accepted instruction in English grammar from Godwin.

2. *Twelfth Night,* II. iv. 114.

3. "Imlay eventually gave a bond for a sum to be settled on his child; . . . but neither principal nor interest was ever paid" (C. Kegan Paul, *William Godwin: His Friends and Contemporaries,* London, 1876, I, 229).

4. Joseph Johnson, the bookseller who published all Mary's books.

32. MARY TO GODWIN
[September 4, 1796]

Sunday Night

I have spent a pleasant day, *perhaps*, the pleasanter, for walking with you first, with only the family, and Mrs. Inch[bald]—We had less wit and more cordiality—and if I do not admire her more I love her better—She is a charming woman!—I do not like her the less, for having spoken of you with great respect, and even affection—so much so that I began to think you were not out in your conjecture[1]—you know what.

I only write now to bid you Good Night!—I shall be asleep before you—and I would leave you a God bless you —did you care for it; but, alas! you do not, though Sterne says[2] that it is equivalent to a—kiss—

Past ten O'clock!

1. That Mrs. Inchbald is in love with him?
2. See the last two paragraphs of the section entitled "La Fille de Chambre (Paris)" in Laurence Sterne's *Sentimental Journey Through France and Italy*.

33. MARY TO GODWIN
[September 8, 1796]

I received an apology this morning from Mrs Newton and of course you did. I should have called on you in my way home, an hour ago, had I not taken it for granted, in spite of my fatigue—and I do not like to see you when I am not half alive.

I want to see you—and *soon*—I have a world to say to you—Pray come to your

Mary

34. MARY TO GODWIN
[September 10, 1796]

Fanny was so importunate with her "go this way Mama, me wants to see Man," this morning that you would have seen us had I not had a glimpse of a blue coat at your door, when we turned down the Street—I have always a great deal to say to you, which I say to myself so kindly that 'tis pity you do not hear me—

I wanted to tell you that I felt as if I had not done justice to your essay,[1] for it interested me extremely—and has been running in my head while other recollections were all alive in my heart—You are a tender considerate creature; but, entre nous, do not make too many philosophical experiments, for when a philosopher is put on his metal, to use your own phrase, there is no knowing where he will stop—and I have not reckoned on having a wild-goose chace after a—wise man—You will ask me what I am writing about—Why, as if you had been listening to my thoughts—

I am almost afraid on reflection that an indistinct intuition on our affection produced the effect on Miss H[ays] that distresses me—She has owned to me that she cannot endure to see others enjoy the mutual affection from which she is debarred—I will write a kind note to her to day to ease my conscience, for when I am happy myself, I am made up of milk and honey, I would fain make every body else so—

I shall come to you to night, probably before nine— May I ask you to be at home—I may be tired and not like to ramble further—Shou[l]d I be later—you will forgive me—It will not be my heart that will loiter—By the bye—I do not tell *any* body[2]—especially yourself—it is alway on my lips at your door—

The return of the fine weather has led me to form a vague wish that we might *vagabondize* one day in the country—before the summer is clear gone. I love the country and like to leave certain associations in my mem-

ory, which seem, as it were, the land marks of affection—
Am I very obscure?

Now I will go and write—I am in a humour to write—
at least to you—Send me one line—if it be but—Bo! to a
goose—Opie[3] left a card last night—

1. Probably one of the essays in Godwin's *The Enquirer*. (See
note 2, Letter 9, above.)
2. Mary and Godwin kept their love affair secret until after
their marriage.
3. John Opie, R.A., who painted Mary's portrait in 1797 and
who was reported to be about to marry her as late as November,
1796. (See *Memoirs,* ed. Durant, p. 312, and cf. Letter 61, below.)

35. GODWIN TO MARY
[undated]

Bo!

Mr. Merry[1] boasts that he once wrote an epilogue to a
play of Miles Peter Andrews,[2] while the servant waited in
the hall. That is not my talent. So, as you once said, I shall
cork up my heart; to see whether it will fly out ce soir at
sight of you.

Saturday

1. Robert Merry, leader of the pretentious Della Cruscan
School of English poetry.
2. Owner of a powder magazine at Dartford and M.P. for
Bewdley, who enjoyed success as a popular dramatist, wit, and host.

36. MARY TO GODWIN
[September 13, 1796]

You tell me, William, that you augur nothing good, when the paper has not a note, or, at least, Fanny to wish you a good morning—

Now by these presents let me assure you that you are not only in my heart, but my veins, this morning. I turn from you half abashed—yet you haunt me, and some look, word or touch thrills through my whole frame—yes, at the very moment when I am labouring to think of something, if not somebody, else. Get ye gone Intruder! though I am forced to add dear—which is a call back—

When the heart and reason accord there is no flying from voluptuous sensations, I find, do what a woman can —Can a philosopher do more?

Mary

37. GODWIN TO MARY
[undated]

I have been a prisoner all this morning. If I do not hear from you, I shall expect you to tea. Dyson[1] dines with me, &, alas! if I do not command him to depart, he would probably stay with me alone till midnight. When you come, I trust he will soon withdraw. Will that do?

He tells me you are in high health & a flow of spirits. Intelligence, how welcome!

Tuesday, 4 o'clock

1. George Dyson, whom Godwin listed with Coleridge, Holcroft, and Joseph Fawcett as one of his "principal oral instructors." (See Paul, *William Godwin,* I, 17.)

38. GODWIN TO MARY
September 14, 1796

Il faut que la visite soit chez moi ce soir, n'est-ce pas? Et à quelle heure?

Je ordonne à vous que vous écrivez ce matin, et avec une génie étonnante! comme assinément vous pouvez si bien.

Mercredi, Sep. 14

39. MARY TO GODWIN
[September 14, 1796]

I have no genius this morning—Poor Fannikin has the chicken-pox—which I am glad of—as I now know what is the matter with her. Business takes me to Mr. Johnson's[1] to day—I had rather you would come to me this evening—I shall be at home between eight and nine; but do not make a point of interrupting any party—I like to be near Fanny till she is better.

1. Joseph Johnson's bookshop at No. 72 St. Paul's Churchyard.

40. MARY TO GODWIN
[September 15, 1796]

The virulence of my poor Fanny's distemper begins to abate, and with it my anxiety—yet this is not, I believe, a day sufficiently to be depended on, to tempt us to set out in search of rural felicity. We must then woo philosophy *chez vous* ce soir, nest-ce pas; for I do not like to lose my Philosopher even in the lover.

You are to give me a lesson this evening—And, a word in your ear, I shall not be very angry if you sweeten grammatical disquisitions after the Miltonic mode[1]—Fancy, at this moment, has turned a conjunction into a kiss; and the sensation steals o'er my senses. N'oublierez pas, I pray thee, the graceful pauses, I am alluding to; nay, anticipating—yet now you have led me to discover that I write worse, than I thought I did, there is no stopping short—I must improve, or be dissatisfied with myself—

I felt hurt, I can scarcely trace why, last night, at your wishing time to roll back. The observation wounded the delicacy of my affection, as well as my tenderness—Call me not fastidious; I want to have such a firm *throne* in your heart, that even your imagination shall not be able to hurl me from it, be it ever so active.

Mary

1. See *Paradise Lost*, IV, 492-502.

41. GODWIN TO MARY
[undated]

I conceived this to be a day fit for our excursion, & regretted its lying fallow; but you know best. I shall expect you.

Thursday

42. MARY TO GODWIN
[September 17, 1796]

My poor Fanny is not so well as I expected—I write with her in my arms—I have been trying to amuse her all the morning to prevent her scratching her face. I am very glad, I did not stay from her last night; for I find she did nothing, but seek for me the morning before and moan my absence, which increased her fever.

Opie called Tuesday evening—from a message, which he left, I am *almost* afraid that the *Devil* will call this evening—

44. MARY TO GODWIN
[September 19, 1796]

I am a little feverish to day. I had full employment yesterday; nay, was extremely fatigued by endeavouring to prevent Fanny from tearing herself to pieces; and afterward she would scarcely allow me to catch half an hour, of what deserved the name of sleep.

I could have wished to have spent a long evening with

you, instead of a flying visit, and I should have been my-self again. Why could you not say *how do ye do* this morn-ing? It is I who want nursing first, you perceive—are you above the feminine office? I think not, for you are above the affectation of wisdom. Fanny is much better to day.

Monday noon

45. MARY TO GODWIN
[September 21, 1796]

Though I am not quite satisfied with myself, for acting like such a mere Girl, yesterday—yet I am better —What did you do to me? And my poor Lambkin seems to be recovering her health & spirits faster than her beauty —Say only that we are friends; and, within an hour or two, the hour when I may expect to see you—I shall be wise and demure—never fear—and you must not leave the philosopher behind—

Wednesday Morning

46. GODWIN TO MARY
[undated]

Friends? Why not? If I thought otherwise, I should be miserable.

In the evening expect me at nine, or a little before.

47. MARY TO GODWIN
[September 28, 1796]

I was detained at Miss Hay's, where I met Mrs Bunn, as it was necessary for me to out stay her. But this is not the worst part of the story. Mrs Bunn was engaged to dine at Opie's, who had promised to bring her to see me this evening—They will not stay long of course—so do as you please I have no objection to your drinking tea with them—But should you not like it—may I request you drink tea with M. Hays, and come to me at an early hour. Nay, I wish you would call on me in your way for half an hour—as soon as you can rise from table; I will then give you the money.

48. MARY TO GODWIN
[September 29, 1796]

It is my turn, William, to be indisposed. Every dog has his day, you know. And, as you like a moral in your heart, let me add, as one applicable to the present occasion, whatever you may think—that there is no end to our disappointments when we reckon our chickens too soon.

I shall be with you at five, to receive what you promised to give me *en passant*—Mais, à notre retour, rien que philosophie. Mon cher ami. Etes-vous bien faché?

Mon Bien-aimé—Moi aussi, cependant la semaine approchant. do you understand me—

49. GODWIN TO MARY
[undated]

Take your tea with me. If you do not like that, let me know.

Man

50. GODWIN TO MARY
[undated]

I am under a necessity of dining out. Thus circumstanced, will you condescend to admit me in the evening at eight or nine?

51. GODWIN TO MARY
[undated]

Will you do me the favor to send Caleb Williams[1] to Mr. Stoddart,[2] No. 6, South Row (opposite Chalton Street) Somers Town? I forgot it last night when I left you.

Adorable maitresse! J'éspère que vous étes plus gai ce matin! Prenez garde à vous!

Saturday

1. Godwin's novel, *The Adventures of Caleb Williams*, published in 1794.
2. Probably John (later Sir John) Stoddart, Hazlitt's wife's brother, who distinguished himself as editor of the *New Times* and Chief Justice at Malta.

52. MARY TO GODWIN
[September 30, 1796]

When there is not a good reason to prevent it I wish you to dine with me, or I with you, of a saturday, to enable *us* to bear the privation of sunday, with philosophie. To morrow is my turn, and I shall expect you. This arrangement renders it necessary to alter the previous plan for ce soir. What say you—may I come to your house, about eight—to philosophize? You once talked of giving me one of your keys, I then could admit myself without tying you down to an hour, which I cannot always punctually observe in the character of a woman, unless I tacked that of a wife to it.

If you go out, at two, you will, perhaps call and tell me that you thought as kindly of me last night, as I did of you; for I am glad to discover great powers of mind in you, even at my own expence. One reason, I believe, why I wish you to have a good opinion of me is a conviction that the strongest affection is the most involuntary—yet I should not like you to love, you could not tell what, though it be a french compliment of the first class, without my explanation of it: the being enamoured of some fugitive charm, that seeking somewhere, you find every where: yes; I would fain live in your heart and employ your imagination—Am I not very reasonable?

You do not know how much I admired your self-government, last night, when your voice betrayed the struggle it cost you—I am glad that you force me to love you more and more, in spite of my fear of being pierced to the heart by every one on whom I rest my mighty stock of affection.—Your tenderness was considerate, as well as kind,

—Miss Hays entering, in the midst of the last sentence, I hastily laid my letter aside, without finishing, and have lost the remain—Is it sunk in the quicksand of Love?

I have now only to say that I go into the city round by Finsbury Square.

If you send me no answer I shall expect you.

Friday

53. MARY TO GODWIN
[October 4, 1796]

So I must write a line to sweeten your dinner —No; to give you a little salt for your mutton, rather: though your not partaking of a morsel, Mary[1] was bring[ing] me up, of this dinner, as you were going out, prevented me from relishing it—

I should have liked to have dined with you to day, after finishing your essays—that my eyes, and lips, I do not exactly mean my voice, might have told you that they had raised you in my *esteem*. What a cold word! I would say love, if you will promise not to dispute about its propriety, when I want to express an increasing affection, founded on a more intimate acquaintance with your heart and understanding.

I shall cork up all my kindness—yet the fine volatile essence may fly off in my walk—you know not how much tenderness for you may escape in a voluptuous sigh, should the air, as is often the case, give a pleasurable movement to the sensations, that have been clustering round my heart, as I read this morning—reminding myself, every now and then, that the writer *loved me*. Voluptuous is often ex-

41

pressive of a meaning I do not now intend to give. I would describe one of those moments, when the senses are exactly tuned by the rising tenderness of the heart, and according reason entices you to live in the present moment, regardless of the past or future—It is not rapture.—It is a sublime tranquillity. I have felt it in your arms—Hush! Let not the light see, I was going to say hear it—These confessions should only be uttered—you know where, when the curtains are up—and all the world shut out—

Ah me! What shall I do to day, I anticipate the un-pleasing task of repressing kindness—and I am overflow-ing with the kindest sympathy—I wish I may find you at home when I carry this letter to drop it in the box,—that I may drop a kiss with it into your heart, to be embalmed, till we meet, closer—[Mary drew a line through *closer* and added the following:] Don't read the last word—I charge you!

1. A servant in Mary Wollstonecraft's household. (See note 3, Letter 9, above.)

54. MARY TO GODWIN
[October 6, 1796]

I was vext, last night, to hear the rain patter, while I was undressing myself—Did he get wet? poor fellow!

Will you give Mary the coat you mentioned, for her boy, if it be not inconvenient. And the corn plaster, for me, should it be at hand.

Are you very gay to day? Gay without an effort—that is best—Fanny won't let me alone—Adieu!

55. GODWIN TO MARY
October 6, 1796

Non: je ne suis pas gai sans effort. The rain fell, but did not wet me; I wore a charmed skin.

If you would have your Latin books cet après hier [*sic*],—Pray bring them here yourself.

Man

6th Octr.

56. MARY TO GODWIN
[October 7, 1796]

The weather has disarranged my plan to day —Will you come and spend the evening with me?—Let me see you, if you please, at an early hour, and I will tell you why you damped my spirits, last night, in spite of all my efforts—Reason may rule the conduct; but even philosophers, I find, cannot command the spirits—yet, we are so happy, sometimes, when we least know why.

Can you solve this problem? I was endeavouring to discover last night, in bed, what it is in me, of which you are afraid. I was hurt at perceiving that you were—but no more of this—mine is a sick heart; and in a life, like this, the fortitude of patience is the most difficult to acquire.

Au revoir—

57. GODWIN TO MARY
[undated]

Mr. Allen[1] has been with me; Mr. Carlisle[2] is coming. I believe his visit will be about three. I wish you did not dine at Mr. Johnson's; at least I wish you could be with me soon after dinner. I suppose they will spoil my dinner.

Do not be alarmed, my love. I am in the gayest health. I believe this boy pupil[3] turns mole-hills into mountains.

William

Monday, 11 o'clock

1. Perhaps the Mr. Baugh Allen mentioned in Letter 130, below.
2. Anthony (later Sir Anthony) Carlisle, surgeon at the West-minster Hospital, who attended Mary in her last illness.
3. Godwin himself (regarded as Mary's pupil)?

58. MARY TO GODWIN
[October 26, 1796]

I think, as an *amende honorable,* you ought to read my answer to Mr. Burke.[1]

Fanny wishes to ask Man's pardon—She won't cry any more.

Are you burnt up alive?

1. Mary's *A Vindication of the Rights of Men, in a Letter to the Right Honourable Edmund Burke* (1790) was a reply to Burke's *Reflections on the Revolution in France.*

59. MARY TO GODWIN
[October 27, 1796]

Mrs. Cotton[1] comes to morrow, should it prove fine, or saturday. She talks of a *few* days. Mon Dieu! Heaven and Earth!

1. A friend of Mary's who lived at the village of Sonning, near Reading, in Berkshire. Mary visited her there in March, when she was struggling to recover from the effects of Imlay's abandonment.

60. GODWIN TO MARY
[undated]

I dine at two: if I were to call on Mr Marshal[1] before dinner, it would devour the whole remainder of my little morning. Yet I want to say to him a few certain words. I wonder how this can be contrived? Can you lend me one of your half dozen servants for this purpose? Can she deliver the inclosed, & wait for an answer? And can the answer, so procured, be permitted to lie on your table till I call in the evening?

1. See note 6, Letter 2, above.

61. MARY TO GODWIN
[November 3, 1796]

If you are not *all alive* at your Essays I will come to you in the course of half an hour—Say the word—for I shall come to you, or read Swift.

You have almost captivated Mrs. C[otton]—Opie called

this morning—But you are the man—Till we meet joy be with thee—Then—what then?

Mary

Thursday Morning

63. MARY TO GODWIN
[November 10, 1796]

I send you your household linen—I am not sure that I did not feel a sensation of pleasure at thus acting the part of a wife, though you have so little respect for the character. There is such a magic in affection that I have been more gratified by your clasping your hands round my arm, in company, than I could have been by all the admiration in the world, tho' I am a woman—and to mount a step higher in the scale of vanity, an author.

I shall call toward one o'clock not to deprive the world of your bright thoughts, this exhilarating day.

Mary

Thursday

64. MARY TO GODWIN
[November 13, 1796]

If the felicity of last night has had the same effect on your health as on my countenance, you have no cause to lament your failure of resolution: for I have seldom seen so much live fire running about my features as this morning when recollections—very dear, called forth the blush of pleasure, as I adjusted my hair.

Send me word that all is safe—and that we are to hear no more of the hard word; though, since I have seen Mr Allen, I should not lay so much stress on it.

The place is to be taken to day. There seem [*sic*] then something like a certainty of freedom next week—are you sorry?

Return me a line—and I pray thee put this note under lock and key—and, unless you love me *very much* do not read it again.

Sunday Morning
Lend me Mrs Robinsson's Poems.[1]

1. Mary ("Perdita") Robinson, former actress and mistress of the Prince of Wales, published her *Poems* in 1775 and 1791 and *Poems, Volume the Second* in 1793.

65. GODWIN TO MARY
[undated]

I have sent one volume of Mrs Robinson's Poems, & at this instant I can not find the other. I hope it is of no moment.

What can I say? What can I write with Marguerite[1] perched in a corner by my side? I know not. I am in health: I do not lament my failure of resolution: I wish I had been a spectator of the live fire you speak of: I *shall* rejoice in our freedom.

Send me the next time anybody comes my bottle of ink:

you can fill an inkstand. Fill it as high, as your image at
this moment fills my mind.

Sunday

1. See note 5, Letter 2, above.

66. MARY TO GODWIN
[November 18, 1796]

How do you do this morning—are you alive?
It is not *wise* to be cold during such a domesticating season,
I mean then to dismiss all my frigid airs before I draw near
your door, this evening, and should you, in your way from
Mr. Carlisle's, *think* of inquiring for the fourth act of Mrs.
Inc[hbald]'s comedy[1]—why it would be a pretty mark of
attention.—And—entre nous, *little* marks of attention are
incumbent on you at present—But—don't mistake me—I
do not wish to put you on your mettle. No; I only want to
secure a play, of some kind or other, to rouse my torpid
spirits, chez vous.

Mary

Friday Morning

1. Probably the manuscript of *Wives as They Were, and Maids as They Are,* which was first presented at Covent Garden on March 4, 1797.

67. GODWIN TO MARY
[undated]

Yes, I am alive. Perhaps I am better. I am glad to hear how enchanting & divine you will appear this evening.—You spoil little attentions by anticipating them.

Friday

68. MARY TO GODWIN
[November 19, 1796]

I wish you would always take my ye for a ye; and my nay for a nay. It torments me to be obliged to guess at, or guard against, false interpretations—and, while I am wishing, I will add another—that you could distinguish between jest and earnest, to express myself elegantly. To give you a criterion. I never play with edged-tools; (I believe) for when I am really hurt or angry I am dreadfully serious. Still allow me a little more tether than is necessary for the purpose of feeding, to keep soul and body together—Let me, I pray thee! have a sort of *comparative* freedom, as you are a profound Grammarian, to run round, as good, better, best;—cheerful, gay, playful; nay even frolicksome, once a year—or so, when the whim seizes me of skipping out of bounds. Send me a *bill of rights*—to this purport, under your hand and seal, with a *Bulletin* of health.

Now I have an inclination to be saucy and tell you that I kissed Fanny, not with less kindness, because she put me in mind of you this morning, when she came crowing up stairs to tell me that she did not cry when her face was washed—I leave you to make the application—

Johnson has sent to inform me that he dines out to morrow; probably with your party.

I was going to close my note without telling you to what particular circumstance the first sentence alludes. I thought of not sending Marguerite to day, because I really felt with respect to her as you imagined I did in the other case, the day before yesterday; but Mary had business for me another way, and I hate to disguise any feeling, when writing or conversing, with you, cher ami.

Saturday Morning   Voila! my resolution—

69. GODWIN TO MARY
[undated]

I can send you a bill of rights & a bill of health: the former *carte blanche;* the latter, Much better (as I think). But to fulfil the terms of your note, you must send me a bill of understanding. How can I always distinguish always between your jest & earnest, & know when your satire means too much & when it means nothing? But I will try.

I have somebody with me, & can write no more.

70: MARY TO GODWIN
[undated]

I do not think myself worse to day—yet, from the appearance of the weather, must determine not to go to the play to night. The heavy clouds promise snow, and I have suffered so much that I have learnt prudence.

What will you do with yourself? ma cher ami—Is there any probability of my seeing you to day? Or, will you confine all your world of love in your own bosom to keep yourself warm? Adieu!

Mary

71. MARY TO GODWIN
[undated]

I am decidedly better to day but I have suffered so much that I must be careful. I think I may venture to go with you to the play to morrow, and then I will renew my acquaintance with your kennel, for which, by the bye, I have *some* kindness.

I do not intended [*sic*] to be out late; yet, as I shall be attended, I must go home, and I cannot well go out again immediately, now I am considered as indisposed, and probably I should only come to cough with you—you may look up at my window for a sign, if you please; but I had almost *rather* you should spend the evening comme autrefois, because I do not like—may I say? to disappoint you—

Our *sober* evening was very delicious—I do believe you love me better than you imagined you should—as for me—judge for yourself—

Fanny will scarcely let me write she is so affectionate, because I breakfasted in bed. I am not well—for holding down my head makes it ache—yet I begin to hope—

72. MARY TO GODWIN
[undated]

The references were, in general, just. I have inserted the few words left out or mistaken. There were a few other observations on the first & second essay.

My pen will not allow me to add any thing kind. This is a day for friends to be together.

73. MARY TO GODWIN
[November 23, 1796]

My cough is still *very* troublesome—so that, I believe, it will be most prudent to stay at home to night—I am sorry I kept you with me last night—and insist on your going without me this evening. I own, for I like to tell the truth, I was a little displeased with you for mentioning, when I was seriously indisposed, your inclination to go—and was angry with myself for not permitting you to follow your inclination—I am now quite well enough to amuse myself—and will dine with you some day next week, to day it would fatigue me, for my head aches with coughing.

Thursday

74. MARY TO GODWIN
[undated]

Half after two.

I mean to call with this note, just to say that finding myself better, and the day clearing up, I might have been tempted to accompany you this evening had you *thought* of tempting me—

75. MARY TO GODWIN
[November 28, 1796]

You tell me that "I spoil little attentions, by anticipation." Yet to have attention, I find, that it is necessary to demand it. My faults are very inveterate—for I *did* expect you last night—But, *never mind it.* You coming would not have been worth any thing, if it must be requested.

I have just written to Mrs R.[1] to say that I cannot go to the play.

I insist on my not preventing you from going this evening to see Milwood.[2] I am not such a child as I thought myself.

Monday Morning

1. Probably Maria James Reveley, Godwin's friend and pupil, who by a later marriage became Mrs. Gisborne, friend of Godwin's and Mary's daughter, Mary Shelley, in Italy.
2. Mrs. Siddons was playing the part of the prostitute Millwood in Lillo's *George Barnwell,* which opened on November 28.

76. MARY TO GODWIN
[December 6, 1796]

I am not well, to day, yet I scarcely know what to complain of, excepting extreme lowness of spirits. I felt it creeping over me last night; but I will strive against it instead of talking of it—I hate this torpor of mind and senses.

Tuesday Morning

77. MARY TO GODWIN
[December 7, 1796]

I want to scold you for not having secured me a better place, because it is a mortification to me to be where I can neither see nor hear. We were thrust into a corner, in the third row, quite as bad as the Gallery—I had trouble enough with my companion without this circumstance; but I am determined to return to my former habits, and go by [my]self and shift for myself—an amusement loses its name when thus conducted.

If you will call on me this morning, and allow me to spend my spite—I will admit you after the play to night.

You and Mrs. I[nchbald] were at your ease enjoying yourselves—while, poor I!—I was a fool not to ask Opie to go with me—had I been alone I should not have minded it—But enough for the present—

Wednesday Morning

78. MARY TO GODWIN
[December 12, 1796]

I increased my cold, or rather cough, yesterday. The dress of women seems to be invented to render them dependent, in more senses than one. Had not Miss M— promised to call for me, even Mrs. Siddons would not have tempted me out to day, though I want winding up. I do not know how you make authorship and dissipation agree, my thoughts are sometimes turned adrift.

I will take care of the two news-paper[s], which contain the debates,[1] if you will let me have them again, with this day's.

1. Evidently Parliamentary debates in which Charles James Fox was involved. (See below, Letter 81.) The subject was probably the war with France, which Fox had opposed ever since its declaration in February, 1793.

79. MARY TO GODWIN
[December 13, 1796]

I thought, after you left me, last night, that it was a *pity* we were obliged to part—just then.

I was even vext with myself for staying to supper with Mrs. R. But there is a manner of leaving a person free to follow their own will, that looks so like indifference, I do not like it. Your *tone* would have decided me—But, to tell you the truth, I thought, by your voice and manner, that you wished to remain in society—and pride made me *wish* to gratify you.

I mean to be with you, as soon as I can, this evening. I thought of calling in my way, at three o'clock—Say shall you be at home; but do not stay at home on that account, unless you intend it, though I do not intend to *peck* you.

Tuesday Morning

80. GODWIN TO MARY
December 13, 1796

I like the note before me better than six preceding ones. I own I had the premeditated malice of making you part with me last night unwillingly. I feared Cupid had taken his final farewel.

Call on me at three as you propose, unless you see me first in Judd Place.[1]

Dec. 13

1. Mary was living at No. 16 Judd Place West.

81. MARY TO GODWIN
[December 18, 1796]

I do not know whether you have sufficient philosophy to read this debate without indignation. I could not, and I love Mr. Fox, for feeling and expressing it in so forcible and so manly a manner—This is what I call humanity—I will own to you that I am hurt when humanity and cruelty are beheld with indifference, as speculative points—I could say more, but of this, however, I am certain that true eloquence is only to be produced by the embodying of virtue and vice.

Shall I see you before you go to dinner, I do not mean to stir out to day. If you intend to call say when, because I do not wish you to come, at the moment of dinner, when you do not dine with me.

82. MARY TO GODWIN
[December 20, 1796]

I send you the work, which **Mr. Dyson**[1] says is "so dear to curiosity." He sent it home, this morning, he tells me, does he tell lies? that lameness prevented his bringing it himself. Fanny says, *perhaps* Man come to day —I am glad that there is no perhaps in the case.—As to other perhaps—they must rest in the womb of time.[2]

Send me some Ink.

1. See note on Letter 37, above.
2. Mary's suspicion that she was pregnant was soon confirmed.

83. MARY TO GODWIN
[December 23, 1796]

Was not yesterday a very pleasant evening?

There was a tenderness in your manner, as you seemed to be opening your heart, to a new born affection, that rendered you very dear to me.

There are other pleasures in the world, you perceive, beside those know[n] to your philosophy.

Friday morning.

Of myself I am still at a loss what to say.—

84. MARY TO GODWIN
[December 28, 1796]

Wednesday

I am not well to day. A lowness of spirits, which I cannot conquer, leaves me at the mercy of my imagination, and only painful recollections and expectations assail me. Should it freeze to night, I believe, I had better have a coach—I would give, more than I ought, not to go—I dare say you are out of patience with me.

85. MARY TO GODWIN
[December 30, 1796]

Unless it rains I mean to dine with Johnson to day, and will be with you in the evening; but shall not tie myself to the hour of ten.

I spent a pleasant day yesterday; only with Opie and Peter.

Friday Morning—

86. MARY TO GODWIN
[December 31, 1796]

I shall dine with Johnson; but expect to be at home between seven and eight.

If you were to get the constant Couple,[1] and bring it with you to read, this evening—would it not be pleasant?

Looking over some of your essays, this morning, reminds me that the one I most earnestly wished you to alter, from the most perfect conviction, was that on Public and private Education[2]—I wanted you to recommend, *Day* Schools, it would obviate the evil, of being left with servants, and enable children to converse with children without clashing with the exercise of domestic affections, the foundation of virtue.

1. Probably George Farquhar's *The Constant Couple; or, A Trip to the Jubilee* (1700).

2. Essay VII of Part I of *The Enquirer* is entitled "Of Public and Private Education." Its concluding paragraph, as printed, reads: "The objections to both the modes of education here discussed are of great magnitude. It is unavoidable to enquire, whether a middle way might not be selected, neither entirely public, nor entirely private, avoiding the mischiefs of each, and embracing the advantages of both. This however is perhaps a subordinate question, and of an importance purely temporary. We have here considered only the modes of education at this time in practice. Perhaps an adventurous and undaunted philosophy would lead to the rejecting them altogether, and pursuing the investigation of a mode totally dissimilar. There is nothing so fascinating in either, as should in reason check the further excursions of our understanding." The paragraph may well have been added as a result of Mary's suggestion; it is missing from Godwin's manuscript version of the essay preserved in the Carl H. Pforzheimer Library and printed in *Shelley and His Circle* (ed. Kenneth Neill Cameron, Cambridge, Massachusetts, and London, 1961, I, 146-150).

87. GODWIN TO MARY
December 31, 1796

You treated me last night with extreme unkindness: the more so, because it was calm, melancholy, equable unkindness. You wished we had never met; you wished you could cancel all that had passed between us. Is this,—ask your own heart,—Is this compatible with the passion of love? Or, is it not the language of frigid, unalterable indifference?

You wished all the kind things you had ever written me destroyed.

Saturday, Dec. 31

88. MARY TO GODWIN
[December 31, 1796]

This does not appear to me just the moment to have written me such a note as I have been perusing.

I am, however, prepared for any thing. I can abide by the consequence of my own conduct, and do not wish to envolve any one in my difficulties.

Saturday Morning

89. MARY TO GODWIN
[January 1, 1797]

The weather is so unfavourable that I find I must have a coach, or stay at home. I was splashed up to my knees yesterday, and to sit several hours in that state is intolerable.

Will you then come to me, as soon as you can; for Mary, after leaving this with you, goes on for a coach.

I am not well—I have a fever of my spirits that has tormented me these two night's past. You do not, I think make sufficient allowance for the peculiarity of my situation. But women are born to suffer.

I cannot bear that you should do violence to your feelings, by writing to Mr. Wedgewood.[1] No; you shall not write—I will think of some way of extricating myself.

You must have patience with me, for I am sick at heart —Dissatisfied with every body and every thing.

My depression of spirits is certainly increased by indisposition.

Sunday Morning

1. Godwin did, however, ask Thomas Wedgwood for a loan of fifty pounds. In a later letter he explained that he had needed the money in order to settle Mary's affairs before marrying her. (See Paul, *William Godwin*, I, 234-236.)

90. MARY TO GODWIN
[January 5, 1797]

I was very glad that you were not with me last night, for I could not rouse myself—To say the truth, I was unwell—and out of spirits. I am better to day.

I shall take a walk before dinner, and expect to see you this evening, chez moi, about eight if you have no objection.

Thursday morning

91. MARY TO GODWIN
[January 12, 1797]

I am better this morning. But it snows, so incessantly, that I do not know how I shall be able to keep my appointment this evening. What say you? But you have no petticoats to dangle in the snow. Poor Women how they are beset with plagues—within—and without.

Thursday morning

92. MARY TO GODWIN
[January 13, 1797]

I believe I ought to beg your pardon for talking at you, last night, though it was in sheer simplicity of heart—and I have been asking myself why it so happen[ed]—Faith and troth it [was] because there was nobody else worth attacking, or who could converse—C— had wearied me before you entered. But, be assured, when I find a man that has any thing in him, I shall let my every day dish alone.

I send you *the Emma,*[1] for Mrs Inchbald supposing you have not altered your mind.

Bring Holcroft's remarks[2] with you, and Ben Johnson—

Friday Morning

1. Paul (I, 242) identifies this as the novel *Emma; or, The Unfortunate Attachment* (London, 1773); but it could as well have been Mary Hays's *Memoirs of Emma Courtney,* which was published late in 1796.

2. Presumably manuscript comments on a piece of work by either Godwin or Mary. Although their friend Thomas Holcroft was a prolific writer, he seems never to have published a book with the word *remarks* as part of its title.

93. MARY TO GODWIN
[January 15, 1797]

I have only a moment to tell you, that I cannot call this morning, and I do not know whether I shall be able to go to Mrs. J. tho' I should be sorry to fail. If the weather be tolerable, or I catch a coach I shall go, and therefore cannot say when;—but probably before the hour you set out, usually. I am not quite so well to day, owing to my very uncomfortable walk, Last night. I was very glad I did not promise to call on you; for I was obliged to undress immediately on my return.

To morrow, I suppose, is out of the reach of fate.

Yours truly
Mary

Sunday

94. MARY TO GODWIN
[January 21, 1797]

I forgot to invite you to dine with me this present Saturday, the 21ᵗʰ of Jany. Still I shall expect you at half past four—so no [more] at present from yours &c—

Mary

Saturday morning

95. MARY TO GODWIN
[January 24, 1797]

Tuesday Morning

I am still an invalid—Still have the inelegant complaint, which no novelist has yet ventured to mention as one of the consequences of sentimental distress. If prudence permit I shall take a walk this morning, and, perhaps, call on you, going or returning; but do not stay at home a moment for me. Should I continue unwell, I believe, I had better spend the evening alone; but you shall hear of me, or see me, in the course of the day.

96. MARY TO GODWIN
[undated]

I am not well this morning—It is very tormenting to be thus, neither sick nor well; especially as you scarcely imagine me indisposed.

Women are certainly great fools; but nature made them so. I have not time, or paper, else, I could draw an inference, not very illustrative of your chance-medley system[1]—But I spare the moth-like opinion, there is room enough in the world &c.

1. The *O. E. D.* defines the noun *chance-medley* as "inadvertency, haphazard or random action, into which chance largely enters," and adds: "*Erroneously* put for pure chance, and for 'a fortuitous medley or confusion.'" Mary seems to have applied this second meaning of the word to Godwin's materialistic philosophy.

97. MARY TO GODWIN
[January 28, 1797]

I was glad that you were not with me last night, for the foolish woman of the house laid a trap to plague me. I have, however, I believe put an end to this nonsense, so enough of that subject.

A variety of things assail my spirits at present, and some of my endeavours to throw off, or rather to extricate myself, by failing, have only given an edge to my vexation.

I shall expect you this evening.

Saturday

98. MARY TO GODWIN
[February 3, 1797]

Friday Morning

Mrs Inchbald was gone into the City to dinner, so I had to measure back my steps.

To day I find myself better; and, as the weather is fine, mean to call on Dr. Fordyce.[1] I shall leave home about two o'clock. I tell you so lest you should call after that hour. I do not think of visiting you, in my way, because I seem inclined to be industrious. I believe I feel affectionate to you in proportion as I am in spirits; still I must not dally with you when I can do any thing else—There is a civil speech for you to chew.

1. Dr. George Fordyce, F.R.S., a native of Scotland, was recognized as one of the ablest students and practitioners of medicine during this period. Mary doubtless went to him on this occasion

for a routine examination before her confinement. After the birth of her child he was called in to attend her, and he remained almost constant in attendance until her death. (See *Memoirs,* ed. Durant, Chapter X.)

99. MARY TO GODWIN
[February 4, 1797]

When I promised to visit you, this morning, you forgot that you had previously mentioned your intention of calling on Fuseli.[1] Only say what you mean to do; and whether my visit is to be to day or to morrow.

I shall, probably invite the Frenchman, to drink a glass of wine, if you say you shall not come to night—

Saturday morning

1. Henry Fuseli, R.A., "Painter of Nightmares" and illustrator of Shakespeare's plays. Mary had cherished a hopeless passion for him before her trip to France in 1792.

101. MARY TO GODWIN
[February 13, 1797]

I intended to have called on you this morning, but for the rain, to beg your pardon, as Fanny says, for damping your spirits last night. Everina,[1] only said, that she was so oppressed by her cold that she could not sit up any longer; but she hoped you would not think her uncivil, especially as she found herself unable to join in the conversation. So you shall seal my pardon when we meet.

Monday Morning

1. Mary's sister Everina Wollstonecraft had given up her position as governess with a family in Ireland and was spending a few days with Mary before going down to Etruria, Staffordshire, as governess to the children of Josiah Wedgwood II.

102. MARY TO GODWIN
[February 14, 1797]

Unless the weather prove very tempestuous, my sister would like to go to the play this evening. Will you come to early tea.

I intended to have called on you this morning—we were shopping and I am weary.

103. MARY TO GODWIN
[February 15, 1797]

I have been prevent[ed] by various little things from calling on you this morning—You must excuse this seeming neglect—do not say unkindness. I write now lest I should not find you at home, to say that Everina will pass to-morrow with Miss Cristall[1] and that I will dine with you—If you please.

1. Probably Ann Batten Cristall, author of *Poetical Sketches* (London, 1795). (See *Memoirs,* ed. Durant, pp. 187-190.)

104. MARY TO GODWIN
[February 17, 1797]

Did I not see you friend, Godwin, at the theatre last night? I thought I met a smile; but you went out without looking round.

We expect you at half-past four.

If you have any business, in the city, perhaps, you will leave a letter, for me, at Johnson's, as it is not perfectly convenient to send Mary. But do not put yourself out of your way, I will try to continue to do it *myself,* should you have had an intention of directing your steps in another.

105. MARY TO GODWIN
[February 21, 1797]

My Sister talks of going to Miss Cristall's tomorrow or next day, I shall not then expect you this evening—I would call on you this morning, but I cannot say when—and I suppose you will dine at Johnson's. The evenings with her silent, I find very wearisome and embarrassing. It was what you said in the morning that determined her not to go to the play. Well a little patience.[1]

I am going out with Montagu[2] to day, and shall be glad by a new train of thoughts to drive my present out of my head.

Tuesday

1. In his *Memoirs* of Mary (ed. Durant, p. 23) Godwin reports that Mary's mother said repeatedly, during her last illness: "A little patience, and all will be over!"

2. Basil Montagu, natural son of the Earl of Sandwich and one of Godwin's young disciples, who later distinguished himself as a barrister and editor of Bacon's writings.

106. MARY TO GODWIN
[February 22, 1797]

Everina's cold is still so bad, that unless pique urges her, she will not go out to day. For to morrow, I think, I may venture to promise. I will call, if possible, this morning—I know I must come before half after one; but if you hear nothing more from me you had better come to my house this evening.

Will you send the 2ᵈ vol of Caleb[1]—and pray *lend* me a bit of indian-rubber—I have lost mine.

Should you be obliged to quit home before the hour I have mentioned—say—

1. Godwin's novel, *The Adventures of Caleb Williams.*

107. MARY TO GODWIN
[March 6, 1797]

Monday

Everina goes by the mail, this evening. I shall go with her to the coach and call at Johnson's in my way home. I will be with you about nine, or had you not better *try,* if you can, to while away this evening. Those to come are our own. I suppose you will call this morning to say adieu! to Everina. Do not knock loud, for a child is born.

108. MARY TO GODWIN
[March 11, 1797]

I must dine to day with Mrs Christie,[1] and mean to return as early as I can; they seldom dine before five.

Should you call, and find only books, have a little patience, and I shall be with you.

Do not give Fanny a cake to-day. I am afraid she staid too long with you yesterday.

Saturday Morning

You are to dine with me on Monday,—remember, the salt-beef waits your pleasure.—

1. The widow of Thomas Christie, who with Joseph Johnson founded the *Analytical Review*. It was at the Christies' house in Paris that Mary first met Gilbert Imlay.

109. MARY TO GODWIN
[March 17, 1797]

And so you goose you lost your supper—and deserved to lose it for not desiring Mary to give you some beef.

There is a good boy write me a review of Vaurien.[1] I remember there is an absurd attack on a methodist Preacher, because he denied the Eternity of future punishments.

Friday Morning

I should be glad to have the Italian,[2] were it possible, this week, because I promised to let Johnson have it this week.

1. A satirical novel by Isaac D'Israeli, father of Benjamin Disraeli. An unsigned review of the book appeared in the *Analytical Review* for March, 1798.
2. Ann Radcliffe's novel of that name. A review of the book by Mary appeared in the *Analytical Review* for May, 1797.

110. GODWIN TO MARY
[undated]

I will call on you & it will not then be too late to determine. I may possibly dine at Robinson's[1] the book seller, & not see you till seven or eight o'clock.

1. George Robinson, his brother John, and his son George Jr., publishers of Godwin's *Political Justice,* were in business at a shop on Paternoster Row.

111. GODWIN TO MARY
[undated]

I will have the honour to dine with you.— You ask me whether I think I can get four orders. I answer with becoming gravity I do not know, but I do not think the thing impossible.—How do you do?

112. GODWIN TO MARY
[undated]

I must write, though it will not be long till five. I shall however reserve all I have to say. Non, je ne veux pas être fâché quant au passé.

Au revoir.

113. GODWIN TO MARY
[undated]

I will do as you please. Shall I come to consult you; or will you call on me?

114. MARY TO GODWIN
[March 31, 1797]

I return you the volumes—will you get me the rest? I have not, perhaps, given it as careful a reading as some of the sentiments deserve.—

Pray send me, by Mary, for my luncheon, a part of the supper you announced to me last night—as I am to be a partaker of your worldly goods[1]—you know!

Friday

1. Mary and Godwin had been quietly married at St. Pancras Church two days before, on March 29.

115. MARY TO GODWIN
[April 4, 1797]

I am certainly not at my ease to day—yet I am better—Will you send Mr Marshall[1] to me and I take it for granted that you mean, and can conv[en]iently, get me my spectacles, before you go to dinner—or I will send Mary.

Tuesday morning

1. See note 6, Letter 2, above.

116. MARY TO GODWIN
[April 8, 1797]

Saturday

I have just thought that it would be very pretty in you to call on Johnson to-day—It would spare me some awkwardness,[1] and please him; and I want you to visit him often of a Tuesday—This is quite disinterested,[2] as I shall never be of the party—Do go—you would oblige me—But when I press any thing it is always with a true *wifish* submission to your judgment and inclination.

Remember to leave the key with us of No 29[3]—on account of the wine.

1. Probably Mary felt embarrassed because her marriage had taken place at a time when she was considerably indebted to Johnson.
2. Mary and Godwin had agreed not to monopolize each other's attentions. They avoided going out together and even tried not to frequent the same places.

3. The house in The Polygon, a many-sided block of houses in Somers Town, where Godwin and Mary settled early in April.

117. MARY TO GODWIN
[April 9, 1797]

Pray don't set me any more tasks—I am the awkwardest creature in the world at manufacturing a letter—

118. MARY TO GODWIN
[April 11, 1797]

I am not well to day my spirits have been harassed. Mary will tell you about the state of the sink &c do you know you plague me (a little) by not speaking more determinately to the Landlord of whom I have a mean opinion. He tires me by his pitiful way of doing every thing—I like a man who will say yes or no at once.

119. MARY TO GODWIN
[April 11, 1797]

I wish you would desire Mr. Marshall to call on me. Mr. Johnson, or somebody, has always taken the disagreeable business of settling with trades-people off my hands—I am, perhaps as unfit as yourself to do it—and my time appears to me, as valuable as that of any other persons accustomed to employ themselves. Things of this kind are easily settled with money, I know; but I am tormented by the want of money—and feel, to say the truth, as if I was not treated with respect, owing to your desire not to be disturbed—

120. GODWIN TO MARY
April 20, 1797

April 20th[1]

I am pained by the recollection of our conversation last night.[2] The sole principle of conduct of which I am conscious in my behaviour to you, has been in every thing to study your happiness. I found a wounded heart, &, as that heart cast itself upon me, it was my ambition to heal it. Do not let me be wholly disappointed.

Let me have the relief of seeing you this morning. If I do not call before you go out, call on me.

1. When Godwin supplied numbers for his and Mary's letters he reversed the order of this and Mary's note immediately following. Although both were written on April 20, Mary's was obviously the later of the two.

2. On the evening of April 19 Godwin and Mary had gone to the theater with Mrs. Inchbald. It was her first meeting with the couple since their marriage, and she took the opportunity to be "base, cruel, and insulting." Doubtless there were repercussions after the Godwins' return home. (See Brown, *William Godwin*, pp. 120-121.)

121. MARY TO GODWIN
[April 20, 1797]

Fanny is delighted with the thought of dining with you—But I wish you to eat your meat first, and let her come up with the pudding. I shall probably knock at your door in my way to Opie's;[1] but, should I not find you, let me now request you not to be too late this evening. Do not give Fanny butter with her pudding.

1. John Opie was painting the portrait of Mary which now hangs in the National Portrait Gallery.

123. MARY TO GODWIN
[May 21, 1797]

I am sorry we entered on an altercation this morning, which probably has led us both to justify ourselves at the expence of the other. Perfect confidence, and sincerity of action is, I am persuaded, incompatible with the present state of reason. I am sorry for the bitterness of your expressions when you denominated, what I think a just contempt of a false principle of action, *savage resentment, and the worst of vices,* not because I winced under the lash, but as it led me to infer that the coquetish candour of vanity was a much less generous motive. I know that respect is the shadow of wealth, and commonly obtained, when that is wanted, by a criminal compliance with the prejudice of society. Those who comply can alone tell whether they do it from benevolence or a desire to secure their own easy [ease]. There is certainly an original defect in my mind—for the cruelest experience will not eradicate the foolish tendency I have to cherish, and expect to meet with, romantic tenderness.

I should not have obtruded these remarks on you had not Montagu called me this morning, that is breakfasted with me, and invited me to go with him and the Wedgwoods into the country tomorrow, and return the next day. As I love the country and think with a poor mad woman, I knew, that there is God, or something, very consoliatory in the air, I should, without hesitation, have accepted of the invitation; but for my engagement with your Sister.[1] To her even I should have made an apology, could I have seen her, or rather have stated that the circumstance would not occur again. As it is I am afraid of wounding her feelings, because an engagement often becomes important, in proportion as it has been anticipated. I began to write to ask your opinion respecting the propriety of sending to her, and feel, as I write, that I had better conquer my desire of contemplating unsophisticated nature, than give her a moments pain.

Mary

Saturday morning

1. Hannah Godwin, a poetess of sorts, who was a London dressmaker.

125. MARY TO GODWIN
[June 3, 1797]

How glad I am that you did not go to day! I should have been very uneasy lest you should have pushed on in the teeth of the weather, laying up a store of rheumatism in your bones—and who knows what effect it might have had on future generations!!!

Have you seen, or heard any thing of Montague?

Saturday Morning

126. GODWIN TO MARY
[June 3, 1797]

I write on the back of Tarleton's address,[1] which you may preserve.—Montagu called this morning. We talk of setting out in an hour or two. I shall appear at the Polygon[2] shortly.

1. Sir Banastre Tarleton was a veteran of the American Revolution and a former Member of Parliament. Godwin and Mary seem to have used his frank for the letters which they exchanged during Godwin's trip to Etruria with Basil Montagu.
2. See note 3, Letter 116, above.

127. GODWIN TO MARY
[June 5, 1797]

Stratford-up, Monday

I write at this moment from Hampton Lucy in sight of the house and park of Sir Thomas Lucy, the great benefactor of mankind, who prosecuted William Shakespeare for deer stealing, & obliged him to take refuge in the metropolis. Montagu has just had a vomit, to carry off a certain quantity of punch, with the drinking of which he concluded the Sunday evening.

Is that the right style for a letter?

We are going to dine today at the house of Mr. Boot, a country farmer, with Dr. Parr[1] & a set of jolly fellows, to commemorate the victory, or rather no-victory,[2] gained last week by the High Sheriff of Warwickshire & the oppositionists, over the Lord Lieutenant & the ministerialists, in the matter of a petition for the dismission of Mr. Pitt and his coadjutors. We sleep tonight at Dr. Parr's, 60 miles from Etruria, at which place therefore we probably shall not arrive till Wednesday. Our horse has turned out admirably, & we were as gay as larks. We were almost drowned this morning in a brook, swelled by the rains. We are here at the house of a Mr. Morley, a clergyman with whom we breakfasted, after a ride of twenty two miles. He is an excellent classic, &, which is almost as good, a clever & amiable man. Here we met Catherine Parr, the youngest, as blooming as Hebe, & more interesting than all the goddesses in the Pantheon. Montagu is in love with her.

We slept the first night at Beaconsfield,[3] the residence of Mr. Burke, 23 miles. The town was full of soldiers. We rose the next morning, as well as to-day, a little after four. We drove about twenty miles to breakfast, & arrived at Oxford, 53 miles from town, about twelve. Here we had a grand dinner prepared for us by letter, by a Mr Horseman, who says that you & I are the two greatest men in the world. He is very nervous, & thinks he never had a day's health in his life. He intends to return the visit, & eat a grand dinner in the Paragon,[4] but he will find himself mistaken. We saw the buildings, an object that never impresses me with rapture, but we could not see the collection of pictures at Christ Church library[5] because it was

Sunday. We saw however an altar piece by Guido,[6] Christ bearing the cross, a picture that I think of the highest excellence. Our escort, one of whom thinks himself an artist, were so ignorant as to tell us that a window to which we were introduced, painted by Jervas,[7] (as they said) from Reynolds, was infinitely superior. We had also a Mr. Swan, & his two wives or sisters to dinner; but they were no better than geese.

And now, my dear love, what do you think of me? Do not you find solitude infinitely superior to the company of a husband? Will you give me leave to return to you again, when I have finished my pilgrimage, & discharged the penance of absence? Take care of yourself, my love, & take care of William.[8] Do not you be drowned, whatever I am. I remember at every moment all the accidents to which your condition subjects you, & wish I knew of some sympathy that could inform me from moment to moment, how you do, & how you feel.

Tell Fanny something about me. Ask her where she thinks I am. Say I am a great way off, & going further & further, but that I shall turn round & come back again some day. Tell her I have not forgotten her little mug[9] & that I shall chuse a very pretty one. Montagu said this morning about eight o'clock upon the road, Just now little Fanny is going to plungity plunge. Was he right? I love him very much. He is in such a hurry to see his chere adorable,[10] that, I believe, after all, we shall set forward this evening, & get to Etruria to-morrow.

Farewel.

1. Samuel Parr, LL.D., was a liberal clergyman and teacher who engaged in many literary controversies. His friendship with

Godwin ended after a sermon which he delivered at Christ Church, Newgate Street, on Easter Tuesday, 1800, attacking Godwin's theory of universal benevolence as expressed in *Political Justice*.

2. On May 29, 1797, Robert Knight, High Sheriff of Warwickshire, received a letter from various freeholders and householders in the county asking him to call a meeting on the 31st "for the purpose of taking into consideration the propriety of addressing the King to dismiss his present Ministers from his councils for ever." At the meeting the Sheriff read a proposed petition and declared the majority of those present in favor of it. The opposition, however, asked the Earl of Warwick, as Lord Lieutenant, to take the chair, and an address expressing confidence in the King was then prepared and approved. The texts of both were published in the issue of *Aris's Birmingham Gazette* for June 5, 1797; but neither petition nor address seems ever to have reached the King.

3. Godwin certainly meant that they stopped at the village of Beaconsfield, not at Edmund Burke's estate there.

4. Though there was such an address, Godwin was probably punning on *Polygon*.

5. The collection, established by the bequest of General John Guise, who died in 1765, was regarded as one of the finest in England. Later scholarship proved, however, that many of the paintings were incorrectly attributed.

6. This painting, the altar-piece at Magdalen College Chapel, is no longer attributed to Guido Reni but merely listed as of the School of Seville.

7. Thomas Jervais, or Jarvis, executed Sir Joshua Reynolds' design for the windows of New College Chapel.

8. Godwin and Mary both assumed that their unborn child would be a boy, who was to be named after his father.

9. Godwin had promised to bring Fanny a mug from the Wedgwood potteries.

10. Montagu was paying court to Sarah, youngest surviving daughter of the first Josiah Wedgwood.

128. MARY TO GODWIN
[Tuesday, June 6, 1797]

It was so kind and considerate in you to write sooner than I expected that I cannot help hoping you would be disappointed at not receiving a greeting from me on your arrival at Etruria. If your heart was in your mouth, as I felt, just now, at the sight of your hand, you may kiss or shake hands with the letter and imagine with what affection it was written—If not—stand off, profane one![1]

I was not quite well the day after you left me; but it is past, and I am well and tranquil, excepting the disturbance produced by Master William's joy, who took it into his head to frisk a little at being informed of your remembrance. I begin to love this little creature, and to anticipate his birth as a fresh twist to a knot, which I do not wish to untie. Men are spoilt by frankness, I believe, yet I must tell you that I love you better than I supposed I did, when I promised to love you for ever—and I will add what will gratify your benevolence, if not your heart, that on the whole I may be termed happy. You are a tender, affectionate creature; and I feel it thrilling through my frame giving and promising pleasure.

Fanny wanted to know "what you are gone for," and endeavours to pronounce Etruria. Poor papa is her word of kindness—She has been turning your letter on all sides, and has promised to play with Bobby till I have finished my answer.

I find you can write the kind of letter a friend ought to write, and give an account of your movements. I hailed the sunshine, and moon-light and travelled with you scenting the fragrant gale—Enable me still to be your company, and I will allow you to peep over my shoulder, and see me under the shade of my green blind, thinking of you, and all I am to hear, and feel when you return—you may read my heart—if you will.

I have no information to give in return for yours. Holcroft is to dine with me on Saturday—So do not forget us when you drink your solitary glass; for nobody drinks wine at Etruria, I take for granted. Tell me what you think of Everina's behaviour and situation;[2] and treat her with as much kindness as you can—that is a little more than her manner, probably will call forth—and I will repay you.

I am not fatigued with solitude—yet I have not relished my solitary dinner. A husband is a convenient part of the furniture of a house, unless he be a clumsy fixture. I wish you, from my soul, to be rivetted in my heart; but I do not desire to have you always at my elbow—though at this moment I did not care if you were. Yours truly and tenderly,

Mary

Fanny forgets not the Mug—

Miss Pinkerton[3] seems content—I was amused by a letter she wrote home. She has more in her than comes out of her mouth—My dinner is ready it is washing-day—I am putting every thing in order for your return. Adieu!

I did not think it necessary to forward T. W.'s[4] letter to you—

1. Cf. *Aeneid*, VI, 258: "Procul, O procul este, profani."
2. Mary's sister was now settled as a governess in the house-

hold of Josiah Wedgwood II. Mary was undoubtedly eager to know how she had reacted to the news of her marriage.

3. This woman, otherwise unidentifiable, was about to cause a crisis in the Godwin family. See below, Letters 140-141, 148, and 153.

4. Thomas Wedgwood's. See Letters 131-132, below.

129. GODWIN TO MARY
[June 7, 1797]

More adventures. There are scenes, Sterne says,[1] that only a sentimental traveller is born to be present at. I sealed my last letter at Hampton Lucy, & set off for Mr Boot's, farmer at Atherston[e], where I expected to meet Dr. Parr to dinner. Our way lay through Stratford upon Avon, where, after having paid our respects to the house, now inhabited by a butcher, in which Shakespear is said to have been born, I put your letter in the post.

But, before we entered Stratford, we overtook Dr. Parr. After a very cordial salutation, he told us that we saw him in the deepest affliction, & forbad our visit at present to his house, though he pressed us to wait upon him upon our return from Etruria. He however went on with us upon his trot to the dinner at Atherston[e]. His affliction was for the elopement of his daughter[2] with a Mr. Wynn, a young man of eighteen, a pupil of the Doctor's, son to a member of parliament, & who will probably inherit a considerable fortune. They set off for Gretna Green on the night of Sunday the 4th. To do the Doctor justice; though in the deepest affliction, he was not inconsolable. He had said to the young man the Friday before, Sir, it is necessary we should come to an issue; you must either quit my

84

house, or relinquish your addresses to Miss Parr: if, after having ceased to live with me, you chuse to continue your addresses, I shall have no objection to you; but I will have no Gretna-Green work: I allow you till Monday to give me your answer. I cannot help however believing that the Doctor is not very sorry for the match. What do you think of it? I certainly regard Miss Parr as a seducer, & have scarcely any doubt that the young man will repent, & that they will both be unhappy. It was her & her mother's maxim, that the wisest thing a young woman of sense could do, was to marry a fool; and they illustrated their maxim from their domestic scene. Miss Parr has now, it seems, got her fool, & will therefore learn by experiment the justice of her maxim.

I expected to have been rallied by the Doctor[3] upon my marriage. He was in high spirits, but abstained from the subject. I at length reminded him of his message by the Wedgwoods. I mentioned it with the utmost good-humour, but desired an explanation, as I was really incapable of understanding it. He appeared confused, said he had been in high good-humour the evening he supped with the Wedgwoods, & had talked away at a great rate. He could not exactly say how he had expressed himself, but was sure he did not use the word mean. We had a good deal of raillery. I told him that he understood every thing, except my system of Political Justice; & he replied, that was exactly the case with me. Montagu afterwards told me, that Dr. Parr had formerly assured him, that I was more skilful in moral science than any man now living. I am not however absolutely sure of the accuracy of Montagu's comprehension.

We left the doctor at the farmer's house, & came on

upon Monday evening to within ten miles of Birmingham
& 50 miles of Etruria. (I forgot to say in its right place,
that Miss Parr vowed, upon hearing of my expedition, that
she would give me the most complete roasting she ever
gave to any man in her life, upon my marriage. She however has got her husband, & I have probably lost my roasting. Though I think it not improbable that we shall find
Mr and Mrs Wynn at Dr Parr's on our return.)

Every night we have ceased to travel at eleven; every
morning we have risen at four; so that you see we have not
been idle. We breakfasted on Tuesday at Birmingham,
where we spent two hours, surveyed the town, & saw the
ruins of two large houses, that had been demolished in the
Birmingham riots.[4] I amused myself with enquiring the
meaning of a hand-bill respecting a wax-work exhibition,
containing, among others, lively & accurate likenesses of
the Prince & Princess of Wirtemberg,[5] & poet Freeth.[6] As
I had never heard of poet Freeth, my curiosity was excited.
We found that he was an ale-housekeeper of Birmingham,
the author of a considerable number of democratical
squibs. If we return by Birmingham, I promise myself to
pay him a visit.

From Birmingham we passed through Walsall, a large
and handsome town of this county, 8 miles. We went forward, however, & came at twelve o'clock to Cannoc[k], a
pretty little town, 8 miles more. Here we proposed giving
our horse some water & a mouthful of hay. Montagu had
repeatedly regretted the hardship imposed upon the horse,
of eating his hay with a large bit of iron in his mouth, &
here therefore he thought proper to take off his bridle at
the inn door. The horse finding himself at liberty, immediately pranced off, overturned the chaise, dashed it against

a post, & broke it in twenty places. It was a formidable sight, & the horse was with great difficulty stopped. We however are philosophers; so, after having amused ourselves for some time with laughing at our misadventure, we sent for a smith to splinter our carriage. By two we had eaten our dinner, the chaise was hammered together, we paid the smith his demand of two shillings, & bid adieu to Cannoc[k], the scene of this memorable adventure.

Our next town was Stafford,[7] which I viewed with unfeigned complacence, as having had the honour of being represented in four successive parliaments by Richard Sheridan. We did not however stop here (8 miles), but proceeded to Stone, (7 more), & nine short of Etruria. Here we took tea, & here I wrote the first 18 lines of this letter. You cannot imagine the state of intoxication of poor Montagu, as we approached the place of our destination. It was little less than madness, but the most kind-hearted madness imaginable. He confessed to me that he had set out from London in extreme ill-humour, from preceding fatigue, & from doubts of the capacity of the horse to perform the journey, in which however he was agreeably disappointed. He added that it was infinitely the most delightful journey he had ever made.

We reached Etruria, without further accident, a little after eight. Our reception appears to be cordial. Tho. Wedgwood however wrote me a letter to prevent my coming which I wish you to forward to Gen. Tarleton for me. His address is No. 4, Little Rider Street, St. James's; is it not? You must not however, till further orders, send me any thing after Saturday, as we shall probably leave this place, before it could arrive. If you hear nothing further from me on that point, I request you to make Mr. Davis, the painter,[8] 91, Chancery Lane, acquainted with this regulation some time on Monday morning, & not before. Farewell, my love; I think of you with tenderness, & shall see you again with redoubled kindness (if you will let me) for this short absence. Kiss Fanny for me; remember William; but (most of all) take care of yourself. Tell Fanny, I am safely arrived in the land of mugs.

Your sister would not come down to see me last night at supper, but we met at breakfast this morning. I have nothing to say about her.

1. See the fifth paragraph of the chapter entitled "The Sword (Rennes)" in Laurence Sterne's *Sentimental Journey Through France and Italy*.

2. Sarah Anne Parr, eldest daughter of Dr. Parr, had eloped with John Wynne, son of Robert Watkins Wynne, of Plasnewydd, Denbigh, Wales.

3. Dr. Parr was only one of many who were amused by the inconsistency between Godwin's recent action and the theories expressed in *Political Justice*.

4. In the Church and King Riots of 1791 a mob had burned the Unitarian chapel and the houses of the clergyman, the scientist Joseph Priestley, and several of his parishioners.

5. Ferdinand Friedrich August, Prince of Wirtemberg, married Albertine, Princess of Schwarzburg-Sondershausen. He became Duke of Wirtemberg in 1797, Elector (thanks to Napoleon) in 1802, and King in 1806.

6. John Freeth seems to have brought out only one volume of poems, *The Political Songster; or, A Touch of the Times, on Various Subjects and Adapted to Common Tunes*. The sixth edition was published by T. Pearson of Birmingham in 1790.

7. Between this and the preceding paragraph two and a half lines have been crossed out and are illegible.

8. Although there were two well-known artists named Davis early in the nineteenth century, neither was established by 1797;

in fact John Philip Davis was only thirteen years old then, and Richard Barrett Davis was fifteen. Godwin may, of course, have been referring to a house-painter by that name rather than an artist.

130. GODWIN TO MARY

Etruria, June 10, 1797

You cannot imagine how happy your letter made me. No creature expresses, because no creature feels, the tender affections, so perfectly as you do: &, after all one's philosophy, it must be confessed that the knowledge, that there is some one that takes an interest in our happiness something like that which each man feels in his own, is extremely gratifying. We love, as it were, to multiply our consciousness & our [?], even at the hazard of what Montagu described so pathetically one night upon the New Road, of opening new avenues for pain & misery to attack us.

We arrived, as you are already informed, at Etruria on Tuesday afternoon. Wednesday I finished my second letter to you, which was exchanged that evening for your letter written the preceding day. This is the mode of carrying on correspondence at Etruria: the messenger who brings the letters from Newcastle under Line, 2 miles, carries away the letters you have already written. In case of emergency however, you can answer letters by return of post, & send them an hour after the messenger, time enough for the mail.

To the letter I now write, I cannot, if we prosecute our plans, receive any answer. Indeed I begin to apprehend, as I write, that it cannot be sent to-day. I wrote last on

Wednesday, a letter, which of course you were to receive this morning. It is probable that you are now reading it: it is between twelve & one. I hope it finds you in health & spirits. I hope you hail the hand-writing on the direction, though not probably with the surprise that, it seems, the arrival of my first letter produced. You are now reading my adventures: the elopement of Mrs Wynn; the little, good-humoured sparring between me & Doctor Parr; and the tremendous accident of Cannock. These circumstances are presenting themselves with all the grace of novelty. I am, at the same time reading your letter, I believe, for the fourth time, which loses not one grace by the repetition. Well; fold it up, give Fanny the kiss I sent her, & tell her, as I desired you, that I am in the land of mugs. You wish, it may be, that my message had been better adapted to her capacity; but I think it better as it is; I hope you do not disdain the task of being its commentator.

One of the pleasures I promised myself in my excursion, was to increase my value in your estimation, & I am not disappointed. What we possess without intermission, we inevitably hold light; it is a refinement in voluptuousness, to submit to voluntary privations. Separation is the image of death; but it is Death stripped of all that is most tremendous, & his dart purged of its deadly venom. I always thought St Paul's rule,[1] that we should die daily, an exquisite Epicurean maxim. The practice of it, would give to life a double relish.

My sentence towards the close of the preceding page is scarcely finished "I wrote last on Wednesday" Thursday I ventured to intermit. To-day is Friday, so, I fear, no post day; since no mail is delivered in London on a Sunday.

Yesterday we dined at Mrs. Wedgwood's the elder;[2]

Everina was not of the party. They sat incessantly from 3 o'clock to eleven. This does not suit my propensities; I was obliged to have a ride in the whisky[3] at five, & a walk at half after eight.

Montagu's flame is the youngest of the family. She is certainly the best of the two unmarried daughters; but, I am afraid, not good enough for him. She is considerably fat, with a countenance rather animated, & a glimpse of Mrs Robinson.[4] Perhaps you know that I am a little sheepish, particularly with stranger ladies. Our party is numerous, & I have had no conversation with her. I look upon any of my friends going to be married with something of the same feeling as I should do if they were sentenced for life to hard labour in the Spielberg.[5] The despot may die, & the new despot grace his accession with a general jail delivery: that is almost the only hope for the unfortunate captive.

To-day we went over Mr. Wedgwood's manufactory: Everina accompanied us, & Mr Baugh Allen;[6] no other lady. For Everina, she was in high spirits. She had never seen the manufactory before. The object of my attention was rather the countenances of the workpeople, than the wares they produced. I explained to her the affairs of the letters, & of the £20 from Mr. Johnson. She says, there was a parcel to have been sent by you, the arrival of which, as she imagined, would have been the proper signal for her to have written again. I found no item of this in my instructions.

Tell Fanny we have chosen a mug for her, & another for Lucas. There is a F on hers, & an L on his, shaped in a garland of flowers, of green & orange-tawny alternately. With respect to their beauty, you will set it forth with such eloquence as your imagination will supply.

We are going this evening, the whole family in a party, to see the School for Scandal represented by a company of strollers at Newcastle under Line.

The reason I desired you not to stop Mr. Davis's communications till Monday next, was that I am desirous to give the painting as little interruption as possible. I shall certainly write again on Sunday or Monday, before we leave Etruria.

It is now Saturday, June 10. 1797. I shall probably write again, before I leave Etruria, which we propose to be on Tuesday. I see I had said that before. Your William (do you know me by that name?) affectionately salutes the trio M, F, & last & least (in stature at least) little W.

1. See I Cor. 15: 31.

2. Mrs. Josiah Wedgwood I, born Sarah Wedgwood, was her husband's third cousin.

3. The two-wheeled carriage in which Godwin and Montagu made their journey.

4. See note 1, Letter 64, above.

5. A fortress near Brünn, in Moravia, which was used as a state prison from 1740 to 1855.

6. Probably a brother of Mrs. Josiah Wedgwood II and Mrs. John Wedgwood, both of whom were of the Allen family of Cresselly, in Wales. Mary and her family were friends of the Allens when she lived in Laugharne.

131. MARY TO GODWIN
[June 10, 1797]

Saturday, half after one o'clock

Your letter of wednesday I did not receive till just now, and I have only a *half* an hour to express the kind emotions which are clustering about my heart, or my letter will have no chance of reaching Gen Tarlton to day, and to-morrow being sunday, two posts would be lost. My last letter, of course you had not got, though I reckoned on its reaching you wednesday evening.

I read T[homas] W[edgwood's] letter—I thought it would be affectation not to open it, as I knew the hand. It did not quite please me. He appears to me to be half spoilt by living with his inferiours in point of understanding, and to expect that homage to be paid to his abilities, which the world will readily pay to his fortune. I am afraid that all men are materially injured by inheriting wealth; and without knowing it, become important in their own eyes, in consequence of an advantage they contemn.

I am not much surprised at Miss Parr's conduct. You may remember that I did not give her credit for as much sensibility (at least the sensibility which is the mother of sentiment, and delicacy of mind) as you did, and her present conduct confirms my opinion. Could a woman of delicacy seduce and marry a fool? She will be unhappy, unless a situation in life, and a good table, to prattle at, are sufficient to fill up the void of affection. This ignoble mode of rising in the world is the consequence of the present system of female education.

I have little to tell you of myself. I am very well. Mrs.

Reveley drank tea with me one evening and I spent a day with her, which would have been a very pleasant one, had I not been a little too much fatigued by a previous visit to Mr. Barry.[1] Fanny often talks of you and made Mrs. Reveley laugh by telling her, when she could not find the monkey to shew it to Henry,[2] "that it was gone into the country."

I supposed that Everina would assume some airs at seeing you—She has very mistaken notions of dignity of character.

Pray tell me the precise time, I mean when it is fixed—I do believe I shall be glad to see you!—of your return, and I will keep a good look out—William is all alive—and my appearance no longer doubtful—you, I dare say, will perceive the difference. What a fine thing it is to be a man!

You were very good to write such a long letter. Adieu! Take care of yourself—now I have ventured on you, I should not like to lose you.

Mary

1. Perhaps James Barry, R.A., who was Professor of Painting at the Royal Academy from 1782 to 1799.

2. Mrs. Reveley's young son.

132. GODWIN TO MARY

Etruria (finished), June 12, 1797

Having dispatched one letter, I now begin another. You have encouraged me to believe that some pleasure results to you, merely from thus obtaining the power of accompanying my motions, and that what would be uninteresting to another may, by this circumstance, be rendered agreeable to you. I am the less capable of altering my method, if it ought to be altered, as you have not dealt fairly by me this post. I delivered a letter of mine to the messenger, but I received none from him in return. I am beginning a fourth letter, but of yours I have as yet, only one.

The theatre, which was at Stoke-upon-Trent, two miles from Etruria, was inexpressibly miserable. The scene was new to me, & I should have been sorry to have missed it; but it was extremely tedious. Our own company, consisting of nine persons, contributed one half of the audience, exclusive of the galleries. The illusion, the fascination of the drama, was, as you may well suppose, altogether out of the question. It was the counterpart of a puppet-show at a country-fair, except that, from the circumstance of these persons having to deliver the sentiments of Sheridan & Shakespear (the School for Scandal, & Catherine & Petruchio) their own coarseness and ribaldry were rendered fifty fold more glaring & intolerable. Lady Teazle was by many degrees the ugliest woman I ever saw. One man took the two parts of Crabtree & Moses. Another, without giving himself the trouble to change his dress, played Careless & sir Benjamin Backbite. The father of Catherine had three servants; &, when he came to the country-house of Petruchio, he had precisely the same three servants to attend him. The gentleman who personated Charles in the play, was the Woman's taylor in the farce, & volunteered a boxing match with sir Oliver Surface in the character of Grumio. Snake, who was also footman-general to every person in the play, had by some means contracted the habit of never appearing when he was wanted, & the universal expedient for filling up the intervals, was for the persons on the stage to commence over again their two or three last speeches till he appeared. But enough of these mummers. Peace be to their memory! They did not leave us in our debt: they paid the world in talent, to the full as well as they were paid in coin.

Which is best, to pass one's life in the natural vegetative state of the potters we saw in the morning, turning a wheel, or treading a lay; or to pass it like these players, in an occupation to which skill and approbation can alone give a zest, without a rational hope of ever rising to either?

Saturday morning our amusement was to go to a place called the Tunnel,[1] a portion of under-ground navigation, about a mile & a half, at the distance of three miles from Etruria. We went in a small boat, which was drawn along by a horse. As we approached the Tunnel, we saw a smoke proceeding from the mouth, which gave it no inadequate resemblance of what the ancients feigned to be the entrance to the infernal regions. We proceeded to about the middle of the subterranean, the light that marked the place of our entrance gradually diminishing, till, when we had made two-thirds of our way, it wholly disappeared. The inclosure of the Tunnel was by an arch of brick, which distilled upon us, as we passed, drops of water impregnated with iron. We discerned our way by means of candles, that we brought along with us, & pushed ourselves along with boat-staves, applied to the walls on either side as we passed. Our voyage terminated, as to its extent, in a coal-pit, of which there are several in the subterranean. We had the two elder children with us, who exhibited no signs of terror. I remarked, in coming out, that the light from the entrance was much longer visible in going than returning; &, indeed, in the latter instance, was scarcely perceived till it, in a manner, burst upon us at once.

The only ladies who accompanied us in this voyage, was Mrs Josiah Wedgwood & Mrs Montagu elect.[2] Here, and at the play, where I contrived to sit next her, I saw more of this latter, than I had yet done. I am sorry to observe that she does not improve upon me.

Another evening, & no letter. This is scarcely kind. I reminded you in time that it would be impossible to write to me after Saturday, though it is not improbable that you may not see me before the Saturday following. What am I to think? How many possible accidents will the anxiety of affection present to one's thoughts? Not serious ones I hope: in that case, I trust I should have heard. But headaches; but sickness of the heart, a general loathing of life & of me. Do not give place to this worst of diseases! The least I can think is, that you recollect me with less tenderness & impatience than I reflect on you. There is a general sadness in the sky: the clouds are shutting round me, & seem depressed with moisture: every thing tunes the soul to melancholy. Guess what my feelings are, when the most soothing & consolatory thought that occurs, is a temporary remission & oblivion in your affections!

I had scarcely finished the above, when I received your letter, accompanying T W's, which was delayed by an accident, till after the regular arrival of the post. I am not sorry to have put down my feelings as they were.

We propose leaving Etruria at four o'clock to-morrow morning (Tuesday). Our journey cannot take less than three days, viz., Tuesday, Wednesday, and Thursday. We propose however a visit to Dr Darwin,[3] & a visit to Dr Parr. With these data from which to reason, you may judge as easily as I, respecting the time of our arrival in London. It will probably be either Friday or Saturday. Do not however count upon anything as certain respecting it, and so torment yourself with expectation.

Tell Fanny the green monkey has not come to Etruria. Bid her explain to Lucas the mug he is to receive. I hope it will not be broken upon the journey.

1. Harecastle Tunnel, built by the engineer Brindley, was a part of the Grand Trunk Canal between the Trent and Mersey rivers.

2. Sarah Wedgwood became engaged to Montagu, but later broke the engagement and remained unmarried to her death. Montagu, whose first wife had died, married Laura Rush in 1801 and, after her death, Mrs. Thomas Skepper.

3. Erasmus Darwin, M.D., was the author of the poem *The Botanic Garden* (1789-91) and grandfather of the scientist Charles.

133. GODWIN TO MARY

June 15, 1797.

We are now at The George in the Tree, 10 miles north from Warwick. We set out from Etruria, as we purposed, at five in the morning, Tuesday, June 13. We bent our course for Derby, being furnished with a letter of introduction to Dr Darwin, & purposing to obtain from him a further letter of introduction to Mr Bage,[1] of Tamworth, author of Man as he is, & Hermsprong. Did we not well? Are not such men as much worth visiting, as palaces, towns, & cathedrals? Our first stage was Uttoxeter, commonly called Utchester, 19 miles. Here we breakfasted. Our next stage was Derby, where we arrived at two o'clock. At this place, though sentimental travellers, we were, for once, unfortunate. Dr Darwin was gone to Shrewsbury, & not expected back till Wednesday night. At this moment I feel mortified at the recollection. We concluded that this was longer than we could with propriety wait for him. I believe we were wrong. So extraordinary a man, so truly a phenomenon as we should probably have found him, I think we ought not to have scrupled the sacrifice of 36 hours. He is sixty seven years of age, though as young as Ganymed,[2] & I am so little of a traveller, that I fear I shall not again have the opportunity I have parted with. We paid our respects, however, to his wife, who is still a fine woman, & cannot be more than fifty. She is perfectly unembarrassed, & tolerably well-bred. She seemed however to me to put an improper construction on our visit, said she supposed we were come to see the lions, and that Dr Darwin was the great lion of Derbyshire. We asked of her a letter to Mr Bage; but she said that she could not do that with propriety, as she did not know whether she had ever seen him, though he was the Doctor's very particular friend.

Thus baffled in our object, we plucked up our courage, & determined to introduce ourselves to the author of Hermsprong. We were able to cite our introduction to Dr Darwin by the Wedgwoods, & our intention of having procured a letter from the doctor. Accordingly we proceeded from Derby to Burton upon Trent, 16 miles. This is a very handsome town, with a wide & long street, a beautiful river, & a bridge which Montagu said was the longest he ever saw in the world. Here we slept, & drank Burton ale[3] at the spring, after a journey of 48 miles. The next morning, between six & seven, we set out for Tamworth, 15

miles. At Elford, eleven miles, we saw Mr Bage's mills, &
a house in which he lived for forty years. His mills are
for paper & flour. Here we enquired respecting him, &
found that he had removed to Tamworth five years ago,
upon the death of his younger son, by which event he
found his life rendered solitary & melancholy. The people
at the mill told us, that he came three times a week walking from Tamworth to the mill, four miles, that they expected him at eleven (it was now nine); & that, if we proceeded, we should meet him upon the road. They told us,
as a guide, that he was a short man, with white hair, snuff-
coloured clothes, & a walking-stick. (He is 67 years old,
exactly the same age as Dr Darwin.) Accordingly, about
a mile & a half from Tamworth, we met the man of whom
we were in quest, with a book in his hand. We introduced
ourselves, &, after a little conversation, I got out of the
chaise, & walked back with him to the mill. This six or
seven miles was very fortunate, & contributed greatly to
our acquaintance. I found him uncommonly cheerful &
placid, simple in his manners, & youthful in all his carriage. His house at the mill was floored, every room be-
low-stairs, with brick, & like that of a common farmer in
every respect. There was however the river at the bottom
of the garden, skirted with a quickset hedge, & a broad
green walk. He told me his history.

His father was a miller, as well as himself, & he was
born at Derby. At twenty two he removed to Elford. He
had been acquainted forty years with Dr Darwin. The
other acquaintances of his youth, were Whitehurst,[4] author
of the Theory of the Earth, & some other eminent man
whose name I forget. He taught himself French & Latin,
in both of which languages he is a considerable proficient.

In his youth he was fond of poetry; but, having some motive for the study of mathematics, he devoted his three hours an afternoon (the portion of time he allotted for reading) to this subject for twelve years, and this employment destroyed the eagerness of his attachment to poetry. In the middle of life, he engaged in a joint undertaking with Dr Darwin & another person respecting some iron works. This failed, & he returned once more to his village & his mill. The result filled him with melancholy thoughts, & to dissipate them he formed the project of a novel, which he endeavoured to fill with gay & cheerful ideas. At first he had no purpose of publishing what he wrote. Since that time he has been accustomed to produce a novel every two years, & Hermsprong is his sixth. He believes he should not have written novels, but for want of books to assist him in any other literary undertaking. Living at Tamworth, he still retains his house at the mill, as the means of independence. It is his own, & he considers it as his security against the caprice or despotism of a landlord, who might expel him from Tamworth. He has thought much, & like most of those persons I have met with who have conquered many prejudices, & read little metaphysics, is a materialist. His favourite book in this point is the Système de la Nature.[5] We spent a most delightful day in his company. When we met him, I had taken no breakfast, &, though we had set off from Burton that morning at six, & I spent the whole morning in riding & walking, I felt no inconvenience in waiting for food till our dinnertime, at two; I was so much amused & interested with Mr Bage's conversation.

I am obliged to finish this letter somewhat abruptly, at the house of Dr Parr, where we arrived Thursday (yesterday) about noon, & found Mr. & Mrs. Wynn, but not the doctor, he having thought proper to withdraw himself on their arrival. It is most probable we shall be in town to-morrow evening, but may possibly not arrive till Sunday.

I should have added to the account of Mr Bage, that he never was in London for more than a week at a time, & very seldom more than fifty miles from his home. A very memorable instance in my opinion, of great intellectual refinement, attained in the bosom of rusticity.

Farewel. Salute William in my name. Perhaps you know how. Take care of yourself!—Tell Fanny that her mug & Lucas's are hitherto quite safe. I hope I shall find that the green monkey has resumed his old station by the time of my return.

1. Robert Bage was a self-educated paper manufacturer who turned novelist at the age of 53 to divert his mind from the loss of £1500 suffered from the failure of an iron factory in which he and Erasmus Darwin were investors.

2. Ganymede, the Trojan prince who became Jupiter's cup-bearer.

3. Burton-upon-Trent was already one of the centers of the brewing industry in England.

4. John Whitehurst, who began his career as a maker of clocks, thermometers, barometers, and the like, eventually became recognized as a distinguished scientist. His most famous work, to which Godwin doubtless refers, was *Inquiry into the Original State and Formation of the Earth* (London, 1778).

5. The famous work of Baron d'Holbach published in 1770 under the pseudonym Mirabaud.

134. GODWIN TO MARY

You cannot imagine any thing like Mr Wynn & his wife. He is a raw, country booby of eighteen, his hair about his ears, & a beard that has never deigned to submit to the stroke of the razor. His voice is loud, broad & unmodulated, the mind of the possessor having never yet felt a sentiment that should give it flexibleness or variety. He has at present a brother with him, a lad, as I guess, of fifteen, who has come to Dr. Parr's house at Hatton, with a high generosity of sentiment, & a tone of mind declaring that, if his brother be disinherited, he who is the next brother, will not reap the benefit. His name is Julius, and John Wynn, the husband, is also a lad of very good dispositions. They both stammer: Julius extremely, John less; but with the stuttering of Julius, there is both an ingenuousness & a warmth, that have considerable charms. John, on the contrary, has all the drawling, both of voice & thinking, that usually characterise a clown. His air is *gauche,* his gait negligent & slouching, his whole figure boorish. Both the lads are as ignorant, & as destitute of adventure & ambition, as any children that artistocracy has to boast. Poor Sarah, the bride, is the victim of her mother, as the bridegroom is her victim in turn. The mother taught her that the height of female wisdom, was to marry a rich man & a fool, & she has religiously complied. Her mother is an admirable woman, & the daughter mistook, & fancied that she was worthy of love. Never was girl more attached to her mother, than Sarah Wynn (Parr.) You do not know, but I do, that Sarah has an uncommon understanding, & an exquisite sensibility, which glows in her complexion, & flashes from her eyes. Yet she is silly enough to imagine that she shall be happy in love & a cottage, with John Wynn. She is excessively angry with the fathers on both sides, who, as she says, after having promised the contrary, attempted clandestinely to separate them. They have each, beyond question, laid up a magazine of unhappiness;[1] yet, I am persuaded, Dr. Parr is silly enough to imagine the match a desirable one.

We slept, as I told you, at Tamworth, on Wednesday evening. Thursday morning, we proceeded through Coleshill (where I found a permanent pillory established, in lieu of the stock), & where we passed through a very deep & rather formidable ford, the bridge being under repair, & breakfasted at the George in the Tree, 16 miles. From thence the road by Warwick would have been 14 miles, and by a cross-country road, only six. By this therefore we proceeded, & a very deep & rough road we found it. We arrived at Hatton about one, &, after dinner, thinking it too much to sit all day in the company I have described, I proposed to Montagu, a walk to Kennelworth Castle, the seat, originally of Simon de Mountfort, earl of Leicester, who, in the reign of Henry the third, to whom he was an implacable enemy, was the author of the institution of the house of commons, &, more recently, the seat of Robert Dudl[e]y, earl of Leicester, the favourite, & as he hoped & designed the husband, of queen Elizabeth, to whom he gave a most magnificent & memorable entertainment at this place. The ruins are, beyond comparison, the finest in England. I found Montagu by no means a desirable companion in this expedition. He could not be persuaded to indulge the divine enthusiasm I felt coming over my soul, while I felt revived, &, as it were, embodied, the image of ancient times; but, on the contrary, expressed nothing but indignation against the aristocracy displayed, & joy that it was destroyed. From Dr Parr's to Kennelworth across the fields is only four miles. By the road, round by Warwick it is nine. We, of course, took the field way, but derived but little benefit from it, as we were on foot, from half after four, till half after ten, exclusive of a rest of about ten minutes. One hour out of the six we spent at Kennelworth, & two hours & a half in going & returning respectively, so utterly incapable were we of finding the path prescribed us.

To day, Friday, as fortune determined, was Coventry fair, with a procession of all the trades, with a female, representative of lady Godiva at their head, dressed in a close dress, to represent nakedness. As fortune had thus disposed of us, we deemed it our duty not to miss the opportunity. We accordingly set out after Breakfast, for Montagu proved lazy, & we did not get off till half after eleven. From Dr Parr's to Warwick is four miles, from Warwick to Coventry ten miles. One mile on the Coventry side of Warwick is Guy's Cliff, Mr Greatheed's.[2] My description of his garden was an irresistible motive with Montagu to desire to visit it, though I by no means desired it. We accordingly went, & walked round the garden. Mr Greatheed was in his grounds, & I left a card, signifying I had done myself the pleasure of paying my respects to him, & taken the liberty of leading my friend over his garden. This delay of half an hour precisely answered the purpose of making us too late for lady Godiva. We saw the crowd which was not yet dispersed, & the booths in the fair, but the lady, the singularity of the scene, was retired.

It is now Sunday evening: we are at Cambridge. Montagu says we shall certainly be in town to morrow (Monday) night. The distance is 53 miles: we shall therefore probably be late, & he requests that, if we be not at home before ten, you will retain somebody to take the whiskey from Somers Town to Lincoln's Inn. If Mary be at a loss on the subject, perhaps the people of Montagu's lodging can assist her.

Farewel. Be happy; be in health & spirits. Keep a look-out, but not an anxious one. Delays are not necessarily tragical: I believe there will be none.

1. After three daughters had been born to John and Sarah Wynne, they separated and she sued for separate maintenance. Her health broke down under the strain of the proceedings, and she died at her father's house at Hatton on July 8, 1810.

2. Bertie Greatheed, one of the Della Cruscan poets, had inherited the famous Guy's Cliffe from his father.

135. MARY TO GODWIN
[June 19, 1797]

Monday, almost twelve

One of the pleasures you tell me, that you promised yourself from your journey was the effect your absence might produce on me—Certainly at first my affection was increased; or rather was more alive—But now it is just the contrary. Your latter letters might have been addressed to any body—and will serve to remind you w[h]ere you have been, though they resemble nothing less than mementos of affection.

I wrote to you to Dr Parr's you take no notice of my

letter—Previous to your departure I requested you not to torment me by leaving the day of your return undecided. But whatever tenderness you took away with you seems to have evaporated in the journey, and new objects—and the homage of vulgar minds, restored you to your icy Philosophy.

You told me that your journey could not take up less than three days, therefore as you were to visit Dr. D[arwin] and P[arr]—Saturday was the probable day—you saw neither—yet you have been a week on the road—I did not wonder, but approved of your visit to Mr. Bage—But a *shew* which you waited to see & did not see, appears to have been equally attractive. I am at a loss to guess how you could have been from saturday to sunday night traveling from C[oventry] to C[ambridge]—In short—your being so late to night, and the chance of your not coming, shews so little consideration, that unless you suppose me a stick or a stone, you must have forgot to think—as well as to feel, since you have been on the wing. I am afraid to add what I feel—Good-night.—

136. MARY TO GODWIN
[June 25, 1797]

I know that you do not like me to go to Holcroft's. I think you right in the principle; but a little wrong in the present application.

When I lived alone I always dined on a sunday, with company in the evening, if not at dinner, at St P's.[1] Generally also of a Tuesday, and some other day at Fuseli's.

I like to see new faces, as a study—and since my return

from Norway,[2] or rather since I have accepted of invitations, I have dined every third sunday at Twiss's, nay oftener, for they sent for me, when they had any extraordinary company. I was glad to go, because my lodgings was noisy of a Sunday, and Mr. J[ohnson]'s house and spirits were so altered, that my visiting him depressed instead of exhilirating my mind.

I am then, you perceive, thrown out of my track, and have not traced another.—But so far from wishing to obtrude on yours,[3] I had written to Mrs. Jackson, and mentioned sunday—and am now sorry that I did not fix on to day—as one of the days for sitting for my picture.

To Mr. Johnson—I would go without ceremony—but it is not convenient for me, at present to make haphazard visits.

Should Carlisle[4] chance to call on you this morning send him to me—But, by himself, for he often has a companion with him, which would defeat my purpose.—

1. I.e., at Joseph Johnson's lodgings above his shop at No. 72 St. Paul's Churchyard.

2. Mary visited the Scandinavian countries in 1795 as business agent for Imlay.

3. Godwin apparently objected to her visiting Holcroft only because they had agreed to avoid meeting, and he considered Holcroft to be his friend rather than Mary's.

4. Anthony Carlisle (see note 2, Letter 57, above) attended Mary during her pregnancy.

137. MARY TO GODWIN
[June 26, 1797]

The weather, I believe, will not permit me to go out to day, and I am not very sorry for I feel a little the worse for my yesterday's walk—or rather confinement at dinner—I have not been able to employ myself this morning, and have ordered my dinner early hoping to make it up in the evening—I send for the paper—and I should ask you for some novel, or tale, to while away the time 'till dinner, did I suppose you had one.

138. MARY TO GODWIN
[July 3, 1797]

Monday morning

Mrs. Reveley can have no doubt about to-day, so we are to stay at home. I have a design upon you this evening, to keep you quite to myself (I hope then nobody will call!) and make you read the play—

I was thinking of a favourite song of my poor friend, Fanny's[1]—"In a vacant rainy day you shall be wholly mine"—&c

Unless the weather prevents you from taking your accustomed walk, call on me this morning, for I have something to say to you.

1. Mary's friend Fanny Blood married a man named Hugh Skeys and settled with him in Lisbon. After the birth of their first child, Mary went out to attend her, and she died in Mary's arms.

139. MARY TO GODWIN
[July 3, 1797]

I have been very well till just now—and hope to get rid of the present pain before I see you. I have ordered some boiled mutton, as the best thing for me, and as the weather will probably prevent you from walking out, you will, perhaps, have no objection to dining at four. Send some more of the letters;[1] and, if you bring *more* with you, we might read them after dinner, and reserve my favourite *act* till we were sure of not being interrupted.

You are to send me yesterday's as well as to day's Paper. Yours truly and kindly—

1. As Letters 140-141 and 143-144 reveal, Mary and Godwin were reading some manuscript letters by a "Mrs. V." lent to Godwin by a man named Addington. It is impossible to identify Mrs. V. Elizabeth Vesey, the Bluestocking, had died in 1791, and her letters might well have been circulating in manuscript. As for Addington, there were two brothers by that name, both prominent in Whig circles and eventually Members of Parliament. The elder of the two, Henry, later occupied several Cabinet posts and became Viscount Sidmouth. The younger, Hiley, was an admirer of Coleridge and would have been more likely to be on visiting terms with Godwin.

140. MARY TO GODWIN
[July 4, 1797]

I am not well—no matter. The weather is such, I believe, as to permit us to keep our appointment—and it may as well be over.

What will you do about Addington?

Let me have the reminder of Mrs. V's letters, when you have finished them, that I may not prevent your returning them, when Addington calls.

To be frank with you, your behaviour yesterday brought on my troublesome pain. But I lay no great stress on that circumstance, because, were not my health in a more delicate state than usual, it could not be so easily affected. I am absurd to look for the affection which I have only found in my own tormented heart; and how can you blame me for taken [*sic*] refuge in the idea of a God, when I despair of finding sincerity on earth?

I think you *wrong*—yes; with the most decided conviction I dare to say it, having still in my mind the *unswervable* principles of justice and humanity. You judge not in your own case as in that of another. You give a softer name to folly and immorality when it flatters—yes, I must say it—your vanity, than to mistaken passion when it was extended to another—you termed Miss Hay's conduct[1] insanity when only her own happiness was involved—I cannot forget the strength of your expressions.—and you treat with a mildness calculated to foster it, a romantic, selfishness, and pamper conceit, which will even lead the object[2] to—I was going to say misery—but I believe her incapable of feeling it. Her want of sensibility with respect to her family first disgusted me—Then to obtrude herself on me, to see affection, and instead of feeling sympathy, to endeavour to undermined [*sic*] it, certainly resembles the conduct of the fictitious being, to whose dignity she aspires. Yet you, at the very moment, commenced a correspondence with her whom you had previously almost neglected —you brought me a letter without a conclusion—and you changed countenance at the reply—My old wounds bleed

111

afresh—What did not blind confidence, and unsuspecting truth, lead me to—my very soul trembles sooner than endure the hundred[th] part of what I have suffer[ed], I could wish my poor Fanny and self asleep at the bottom of the sea.

One word more—I never blamed the woman for whom I was abandoned.[3] I offered to see, nay, even to live with her, and I should have tried to improve her. But even she was deceived with respect to my character, and had her scruples when she heard the truth—But enough of the effusions of a sick heart—I only intend[ed] to write a line or two—

The weather looks cloudy; but it is not necessary immediately to decide.

1. Mary Hays made no secret of the disappointment in love which she had suffered. See note 1, Letter 5, above.

2. The Miss Pinkerton mentioned in Letter 128, above. Godwin had seen a good deal of her before and after his trip to Etruria. (See *Shelley and His Circle*, I, 183.) For the sequel to the affair, see Letters 148 and 153, below.

3. According to Godwin (*Memoirs*, ed. Durant, p. 90), Mary even suggested that Imlay take a house and install both her and his new mistress in it.

141. GODWIN TO MARY
[July 4, 1797]

I have not finished the news paper. I do not mean to return the letters to Addington to day. I am much hurt at your note; but Mr. Fell[1] is with me, & I cannot answer it.

1. Ralph Fell, a friend of Godwin and author of *Tour Through the Batavian Republic* (1801). Lamb said of him that he was "the inevitable shadow of everything which Godwin does" (*Letters of Charles and Mary Lamb*, ed. E. V. Lucas, London, 1935, I, 289).

142. MARY TO GODWIN
[July 7, 1797]

Opie has just been here to put me off till Sunday, papa. Should the morning prove favourable have you any objection to calling with me, by way of sparing my blushes, on Mrs. Carr—& Nichcolson[1] [*sic*].

Remember that I have no particular desire to interfere with your convenience—only say the word.

I have just recollected that Sir R. Smith is to set out to day—Had you not better forward your letter, for Miss W—[2] under cover to him immediately.—

1. William Nicholson, the scientist and inventor who a few weeks later was to write a physiognomical analysis of Mary's baby daughter. The letter is reprinted in Kegan Paul, *William Godwin*, I, 289-290.

2. Possibly Mary's sister Everina.

143. GODWIN TO MARY
[July 7, 1797]

I obey, with a pious & chearful obedience, & will be ready to squire you to Thornhaugh & Newman Street[1] at any hour you shall appoint. Sir Rob. Smyth told me he should set out on Tuesday: if you will tell me how you come to know of his having delayed his journey, I should eagerly make use of his conveyance. Send me an answer to these two questions. Send me also the Fair Syrian,[2] & as many of Mrs V's letters as you have entirely done with.

1. Nicholson's letter referred to in the note to Letter 142, above, was dated from Newman Street. Probably the Mrs. Carr mentioned in that letter lived on Thornhaugh Street.
2. A novel by Robert Bage published in 1788.

144. MARY TO GODWIN
[July 7, 1797]

Don't laugh at me—I saw the letter and thought today Tuesday—

I shall be ready at half past two—Between then and three I shall expect you—Have you now sent me all Mrs. V's letters? You forgot that I wished to see the one addressed to you—I have been very much affected by her account of one scene with her husband.—

145. MARY TO GODWIN
[July 13, 1797]

Send me the Fair Syrian—That is the first volume, if you have not finished it. I still feel a little fatigue from my walk—

146. GODWIN TO MARY
[July 15, 1797]

I thought you expressed yourself unkindly to me in the beginning last night. I am not conscious of having deserved it. But you amply made up your injustice, in what followed; & I was tranquil & easy. To day you have called on me, & said two or three grating things. Let me intreat you, not to give me pain of this sort, without a determined purpose, & not to suppose that I am philosopher enough not to feel it. I would on no account willingly do any thing to make you unhappy.

Saturday

147. MARY TO GODWIN
[July 15, 1797]

Mr. Johnson goes to Dorking to day, of course will not dine with us to morrow.

I invited the Fenwicks[1] to drink tea with us to morrow —They had mentioned to you an intention of coming to day—and I wished to put it off. But you may be free notwithstanding.

I do not quite understand your note—I shall make no comments on the *kindness* of it, because I ought not to expect it according to my ideal—You say "WITHOUT a determined purpose." Do you wish me to have one?

1. John Fenwick, supposedly the original of Ralph Bigod in Lamb's "Two Races of Men," and his wife Eliza. Both were authors of sorts, and both assisted with the care of Mary in her final illness.

148. MARY TO GODWIN
[July 18, 1797]

I have thought more of it, and think that I ought to write on the subject which gave me some pain,[1] at first. I should only wish you so far to allude to it, as to convince her that we coincide in opinion.

I am very well—and will walk to Kearsley's[2]—

Say when?

1. That is, the trouble about Miss Pinkerton.
2. George Kearsley, the bookseller, had died in 1790, but his shop on Fleet Street continued in business.

149. MARY TO GODWIN
[July 23, 1797]

If it interfere with no previous plan will you accompany me, before dinner, the later the better, to see those Stupid Carrs?

Do not suppose it is necessary to go with me, for I only want to go because I ought—and such a *motive* will not spoil by keeping.

Fine morality!

150. GODWIN TO MARY
[July 23, 1797]

I think it not right, mama, that you should walk alone in the middle of the day. Will you indulge me in the pleasure of walking with you?

116

I had written the above, before you sent. I will call on you presently.

151. MARY TO GODWIN
[July 31, 1797]

Saddlers-Wells has been the breakfast
day is cool, and we may as well not wear out
If it be convenient to you—determine—and
hour we must time to have sufficient time
slowly, and have a few minutes to rest, pre
commencement.[1]

1. This letter has been badly mutilated. I print all that remains of it, as aligned in the manuscript.

152. GODWIN TO MARY
[August 1, 1797]

I forgot to tell you that I intend, if the weather favour me, to dine at Johnson's to-day. Do you know any reason why I should not?

MARY TO GODWIN [on the same sheet as the above].

No—But you will remember that you have an engagement with a Dame ce soir.—

153. MARY TO GODWIN
[August 9, 1797]

If you find nothing *objectionable* in the enclosed note put a wafer in it, and send it by Mary. I do not now feel the least resentment, and I merely write, because I expect to see her to day or to morrow, and truth demands that I should not seem ignorant of the steps she takes to extort visits from you.

If you have the slightest wish to prevent my writing at all—say so—I shall think you actuated by humanity, though I may not coincide in opinion, with respect to the measures you take to effect your purpose.

Wednesday Morning

[The enclosure:]

Miss Pinkerton, I forbear to make any comments on your strange behaviour [Godwin crossed out the last two words and substituted "incomprehensible conduct"]; but, unless you can determine to behave with propriety, you must excuse me for expressing a wish not to see you at our house.

Mary Godwin

Wednesday Morning[1]

1. The Abinger Collection contains also a note obviously written in reply to Mary's:

At length I am sensible of the impropriety of my conduct. Tears and communication afford me relief

N Pinkerton

Saturday
July 10

The date of the letter is almost certainly erroneous, since July 10,

1797, was a Monday rather than a Saturday. Probably the correct date would be August 10, the day following Mary's note to Godwin, although it too was not a Saturday.

154. GODWIN TO MARY
[August 9, 1797]

I am fully sensible of your attention in this matter, & believe you are right. Will you comply one step further, & defer sending your note till one or two o'clock? The delay can be of no consequence, & I like to have a thing lay a little time on my mind before I judge.

157. MARY TO GODWIN
[August 19, 1797]

I send you Addington's Letters. I find the melancholy ones the most interesting—There is a grossness in the raptures from which I turn—They excite no sympathy—Have no voluptuousness for me.—

Fanny promises to return at your bidding—and would not be said nay—

158. MARY TO GODWIN
[August 30, 1797]

I have no doubt of seeing the animal[1] to day; but must wait for Mrs Blenkinsop[2] to guess at the hour—I have sent for her—Pray send me the news paper—I wish I had a novel, or some book of sheer amusement, to excite curiosity, and while away the time—Have you any thing of the kind?

1. This and the following two notes were written on the day when Mary's second daughter, Mary Wollstonecraft Godwin, was born. The mother died of puerperal fever on September 10 and was buried five days later in St. Pancras Churchyard. Her body was later moved to the Shelley family plot in Bournemouth.

2. A midwife from the Westminster Lying-in Hospital whom Mary had engaged to attend her in her confinement.

159. MARY TO GODWIN
[August 30, 1797]

Mrs. Blenkensop tells me that Every thing is in a fair way, and that there is no fear of the event being put off till another day—Still, *at present,* she thinks, I shall not immediately be freed from my load—I am very well—Call before dinner time, unless you receive another message from me—

160. MARY TO GODWIN
[August 30, 1797]

Mrs. Blenkinsop tells me that I am in the most natural state, and can promise me a safe delivery—But that I must have a little patience

Appendix

A. GODWIN TO MARY
[undated]

I shall not believe you do not hate me, if you do not sometimes call upon me.

(There is, obviously, no specific internal evidence by means of which one can date this unnumbered letter. However, the references to "hate" and to Mary's failure to call suggest that it might have been one of the series which passed between Godwin and Mary on August 17, 1796—possibly the missing No. 16. In No. 13 Godwin writes, "Do not hate me"—the only suggestion of such a feeling in the whole correspondence. In No. 15 he expresses concern at Mary's distress, then relief that she has called on him.)

B. MARY TO GODWIN
[undated]

You will not forget that we are to dine at four. I wish to be exact, because I have promised to let Mary go and assist her brother, this afternoon. I have been tormented all this morning by Puss, who has had four or five fits. I could not perceive what occasioned them, and took care that she should not be terrified. But she flew up my chimney, and was so wild, that I thought it right to have her drown. Express concern to Lucas. Fanny imagines that she was sick—and ran away.

(This letter appears, without date or number, immediately after No. 106 among the Abinger Manuscripts. Godwin apparently regarded it as a continuation of that note, and Kegan Paul so reprinted it in *William Godwin: His Friends and Contemporaries*

(I, 243). However, the two were obviously written with different pens, each bears the mark of a separate seal and is separately addressed to "Mr Godwin," and the two present conflicting plans for the day ahead.

Mary's reference to "my chimney" suggests that this note was written before she and Godwin settled at The Polygon in April, 1797; but there is no internal evidence which would date it more specifically.)

INDEX

123

Stoddart, Sir John, 39
Swan, Mr., 80
Swift, Jonathan, 45

Tarleton, Sir Banastre, M.P., 78, 87,
  93
Twiss, Francis, 11-12, 25, 108

Vesey, Elizabeth, 110
Virgil, 82-83

Wedgwood family, 6, 77, 85, 99
Wedgwood, Mrs. John, 92
Wedgwood, Josiah I, 81
Wedgwood, Mrs. Josiah I, 90, 92
Wedgwood, Josiah II, 67, 84, 91
Wedgwood, Mrs. Josiah II, 92, 97
Wedgwood, Sarah, 80-81, 91, 97-98
Wedgwood, Thomas: lends WG £50,
  61; letter to WG, 83-84, 87, 93, 97
Whitehurst, John, 100, 102
Wirtemberg, Albertine, Princess of,
  86, 88
Wirtemberg, Ferdinand Friedrich Au-
  gust, Prince of, 86, 88
Wollstonecraft, Mrs. Edward, 68
Wollstonecraft, Everina: visits MW,
  66-67, 68, 69; at Wedgwoods', 83-
  84, 88, 91, 94; mentioned, 113

Wollstonecraft, Mary: first meeting
  with WG, 1; love for Fuseli, 2;
  visit to Paris, 1-2, 3; affair with
  Imlay, 3, 70, 112; birth of daughter Fanny, 3; suicide attempts, 3;
  visit to Scandinavia, 3, 107-08; sees
  WG at M. Hays's, 1-2, 3, 4; moves
  to Pentonville, 4; calls on WG, 4;
  moves to Judd Place, 5, 56; becomes WG's mistress, 5, 15-20;
  pregnancy, 5, 57; settles at The
  Polygon, 74; portrait painted by
  Opie, 76, 113; birth of daughter
  Mary, 6, 120; last illness and death,
  6-7, 120
—Analytical Review, contributions to,
  1, 22; Letters to Imlay, 7; Letters
  from Sweden . . ., 4; Mary, 13;
  Posthumous Works, 10; Rights of
  Men, 1, 44; Rights of Woman, 2;
  Wrongs of Woman; or Maria, 10,
  24
Wynne, John: elopes with S. A. Parr,
  84-86, 88, 102, 103-04; separation,
  106
Wynne, Julius, 103
Wynne, Robert Watkins, 88
Wynne, Sarah Anne (Parr): elope-
  ment, 84-86, 88, 90, 93, 102, 103-
  04; separation and death, 106